STOPPING THE
ROLLER
COASTER

STOPPING THE ROLLER COASTER

The Ups and Downs of Depression
and Manic Depression

SHELLEY WALDAIAS

TATE PUBLISHING
AND ENTERPRISES, LLC

Stopping the Roller Coaster
Copyright © 2013 by Shelley Waldaias. All rights reserved.

This book is designed to provide accurate and authoritative information with regard to the subject matter covered. This information is given with the understanding that neither the author nor Tate Publishing, LLC is engaged in rendering legal, professional advice. Since the details of your situation are fact dependent, you should additionally seek the services of a competent professional.

The opinions expressed by the author are not necessarily those of Tate Publishing, LLC.

Published by Tate Publishing & Enterprises, LLC
127 E. Trade Center Terrace | Mustang, Oklahoma 73064 USA
1.888.361.9473 | www.tatepublishing.com

Tate Publishing is committed to excellence in the publishing industry. The company reflects the philosophy established by the founders, based on Psalm 68:11,
"The Lord gave the word and great was the company of those who published it."

Book design copyright © 2013 by Tate Publishing, LLC. All rights reserved.
Cover design by Rtor Maghuyop
Interior design by Jomar Ouano

Published in the United States of America

ISBN: 978-1-62510-245-4
1. Psychology / Psychopathology / Bipolar Disorder
2. Biography & Autobiography / Personal Memoirs
13.04.23

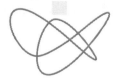

DEDICATION

To my friend Susan, who first inspired me to write this book and for patiently waiting twelve years for it to become reality, thank you for your vision.

To my husband Gordon for his encouragement, understanding, love, and laughter throughout not only the writing of this book but throughout every day of our life together, thank you for your unconditional love.

And to my children, Melissa and Steve, for being strong enough to become your own unique persons. I love you both "infinity."

Contents

INTRODUCTION

The book you're holding is something of a miracle. As a work in progress for over a decade, it's long overdue for being finished. On the other hand, it could be that it is finished at just the right time.

I'm not writing this as a medical or mental health professional but as a woman of faith who happens to live with a mental illness. It's been quite a ride, and more times than I can count, I've wanted to shout, "Stop the ride. I want to get off!"

Oh, before I forget to mention, bipolar disorder and manic depression are essentially the same thing. Bipolar disorder is the clinical diagnosis for what most of us call manic depression.

My personal journey through the jungle of bipolar symptoms is an ongoing expedition. Consequently, putting some of what I've learned into book form has become a journey in itself. Much of what I share with you are the personal discoveries and trial-and-error experiences that I've at times tripped over, stumbled upon, and/or bumped into on my journey. Since being diagnosed with bipolar disorder type

2 back in the mid-nineties, there has been much adjusting and readjusting to find tools and strategies that allow me to not only exist but to truly live a fulfilling and functional life with an invisible handicap. There will never be an absolute formula for 100 percent success in doing that; life is just not predictable enough with its ever-changing landscape of experiences and circumstances. However, I have discovered some practical basics that have proved to be of consistent help in my symptom management. There will always be tweaking and fine-tuning. That's life—the glory and frustration of life. Life is unpredictable and ever-changing. We can choose to embrace that reality and be enriched as a result, or resist it and become embittered by it. I've chosen to embrace it, and I hope that within these pages, you'll be inspired and encouraged to do the same.

It was a purposeful decision to avoid overly organizing the sequence of chapters, choosing instead to share in a more random manner. This book is not intended to be a sequential how-to guide, but something you, the reader, can pick up and open up at random, with each chapter able to stand on its own. It was also a conscious choice to keep each chapter brief. Reading this book should be something that does not intimidate or deter you, the reader, with an overload of words but rather something you will be drawn to by its brevity.

What you find within these pages is, of course, nowhere near to being a complete guide to depression symptom management. It's just some of the highlights of my own journey that I believe could be helpful to others as well. So whether you or someone you know struggles with depression and/or manic depression, it is my hope that in the pages of this little book, you will find insights and practical help—and more than just a couple of smiles along the way.

Blessings to each of you.

EIGHT MONTHS ON THE SOFA

My Own Story in Brief

It was 1991 and I was living my version of the American dream.

I was happily married to a man whose career had advanced, allowing me to be a stay-at-home mom—something that had been my personal dream for years. In 1991, we had two children, a dog and a cat, drove a late-model car, and lived in a lovely new home on a quiet cul-de-sac.

I was involved in church and community activities and connected with others who shared my interests and beliefs. I enjoyed spending time with others and was able to develop good friendships that provided me times of laughing, times of crying, and times of sharing the ups and downs of life.

I was physically active and fit...and loving it—no small feat for someone who grew up being satisfied to have my primary form of exercise be walking from the house to the car and from the car to the destination of choice, then back in the car, heading home.

Most importantly, I had—and have—an authentic and growing spiritual life. My personal relationship with God, my heavenly Father, through the saving grace of Jesus Christ is blessed by the presence of his Holy Spirit, making my faith not just the foundation and framework of my life but the very breath of my life.

Of course, there were struggles. And yes, I was carrying around some pretty hefty emotional baggage with my initials firmly carved into them. But looking back at my life during that time, my life was good—very, very good. Looking in from the outside, some might even say perfect.

So why was I depressed?

But wait…I'm getting ahead of myself because in reality, for most of those eight months on the sofa, I had no idea I was depressed.

I didn't feel depressed.

I felt overwhelmed.
I felt tired.
I felt irritable.
I cried…a lot.

I'd forget the simplest things like shampooing my hair while taking a shower.

Sometimes it felt like I might be having a heart attack.

Sometimes it felt like someone had a strangle hold around my neck and wouldn't let go.

I had barely enough energy to make it through even the most undemanding days.

And whenever possible, I'd spend as much of my day as possible on the sofa, doing nothing.

But I didn't feel depressed.

Back in 1991, along with a whole lot of others, I thought of depression as simply an emotion. It was feeling blue, feeling sad. It was something that, with the right attitude, anybody should be able to just snap out of. Well, I sure couldn't snap out of whatever it was that was essentially robbing me of my life. It didn't even occur to me that I was depressed. Besides, I'm an optimist, and optimists don't get depressed...or do they?

I continued dragging myself through each day without a clue as to how to change it. That is until one day when I was sitting on the sofa as usual and just happened to read a magazine article about clinical depression. I don't remember anything specific about the article except that the author seemed to be writing about me in every paragraph. Did that mean I was depressed like the article was suggesting?

After being encouraged by my wise-beyond-her-years ten-year-old daughter to do what the article said and go see my doctor, I did just that and was officially diagnosed with clinical depression. His advice was that I make an appointment with a counselor to see if medication would help me. That was not a pleasant thought and made even worse when my then husband cautioned me to not talk to the counselor about my family because then "they'll know you really are crazy." And with that one statement, my deepest fears were confirmed. I'm crazy, and I come from a family of crazies.

Not surprisingly, I didn't make an appointment. Instead, I just continued to barely survive each day, doing my best to hide my ugly secret from the outside world.

Knowing only that I hadn't been feeling well for quite a while, our pastor and his wife reached out to me in loving concern. Somehow, I managed to have enough courage to be honest and share what was really going on with me. The very next Sunday, unbeknownst to me, my pastor asked the congregation to pray for me and my health. He was gracious and did not go into any more detail than that. Two days later, I was well. The depression with all its symptoms was gone.

A coincidence? I don't think so. More like a miracle. In retrospect, I wonder how long I would have continued my sofa existence without the prayers of caring people. I am forever grateful for that miraculous escape from the eight-month-long grip of depression.

However, as I was to learn, that miracle was not the end of a story, but the beginning of one.

BUT I DON'T FEEL DEPRESSED

Recognizing Early Warning Signs

One of the most important symptom management tools is learning to recognize your own early warning signs. You might be saying, "What early warning signs?" or "I don't think I have any early warning signs. I'm fine one day and then at the bottom of the pit the next." Those are things that I've actually said. More often than not, it would seem as though everything's going along just fine until without warning, bam! I'm depressed. That is, until I began recognizing a pattern of predictable little signs that something dark was brewing, and I don't mean coffee. It's often a sizeable surprise when we connect the dots and discover our episodes of major depression have early warning signs.

Many times it takes someone else to help us connect those dots. If you have a healthy relationship with someone who has seen you through the comings and goings of bouts with depression, they can often be a great help in identifying those little signs. My sister helped me recognize one of my very predictable signs—one that I've yet to see in any self-help book.

When I'm not depressed, I wake up every morning with some sort of song in my head, usually just a line or two, but it's there and often continues throughout a good portion of the morning. It can be a commercial jingle, a song from grade school, something from a musical, or a worship song. I've learned that if I *don't* wake up with the song of the day playing in my head, I need to make a mental note of that. Then, if there's a second day or more in a row, as my sister pointed out and past patterns have confirmed, I'm well on my way to experiencing a depressive episode. I don't think I ever would've made the connection without my sister's input.

The sooner we pick up on those little nibbles of depression and take steps to stop the darkness from growing, the more quickly and easily the symptoms will be gone.

In some ways, it's not all that different from dealing with a headache. Years ago, I had my doctor tell me that taking a pain reliever after the headache was in full swing was as helpful as putting on an asbestos glove *after* putting my hand in the fire. I realize that he was probably exaggerating to a degree, but his point was made, and I've never forgotten the analogy. It's very much the same with depression. Early awareness—and doing what you know has a good chance of helping stop the downward slide—is a great way to avoid the full-blown pain and darkness of depression...or at the very least, minimize its impact on your life.

I would be naïve and less than honest if I led you to believe that this is some sort of guarantee against a major episode of depression. There may be times when even doing all we know to do, the darkness refuses to budge. Even so, the greater possibility is that we will be able to decrease how often and/or how deep we fall into that black pit called depression.

What I've also learned from my own experience is that the single most challenging aspect in recognizing early warning signs and doing something about it is...denial.

There...I've said it. The *D* word.

Whether or not it's been six weeks, six months, or even a year or more since the last time you were caught in depression's claws, the thought of if it happening again will most likely nudge its way or jump into your consciousness with a significant amount of dread. And dread, my dear friend, is just fear in a different flavor. And fear is depression's ally.

I can't begin to count the number of times, even after learning what my primary early warning signs are, that I've played the "I'm not getting depressed. I'm not getting depressed" broken record in my head.

Denial can even sometimes sound as innocent as "I wonder if I'm getting depressed. I'm not sure if I am or not. Maybe I'm not really getting depressed."

My psychiatrist gave me a good rule of thumb: if you think you might be, you probably are, and it would be wise to take some steps to help yourself break loose of it before it goes any further. Hopefully, that doesn't sound really bleak and distressing. Because as it turns out, when I've chosen to follow her advice, I've been able to short-circuit many of the times that could have become a lot more...well...depressing.

It's perfectly sane to want to avoid depression, but thinking we can avoid it by denying its first or second or third whispers, *never* works.

Even though I've never heard of, or personally experienced, an episode of depression that just exploded overnight, I'm not saying it can't happen that way. But the huge, huge, huge likelihood is that it will come sneaking into our daily routines instead.

That's actually a very encouraging reality because as we learn to notice depression's little tiptoeing early warnings, we are able to become less the victim and more in charge of the quality of our daily existence. What taking charge looks like varies from person to person, but my hope is that as you continue reading this little book, you will have many lightbulb moments for your own personal strategies.

Here are some of the more common early warning signs that can often grow until you are undeniably depressed:

- a growing unwillingness to ask for things
- becoming more down on yourself
- becoming irritable and impatient
- growing feelings of insecurity
- difficulty concentrating
- craving carbs
- not eating
- using repetitive words or actions
- pessimism
- paranoia
- having a hard time getting out of bed
- changing sleep patterns for no apparent reason
- finding that you are using poor judgment
- having obsessive thoughts
- growing misperceptions regarding people or situations
- risk-taking
- avoiding crowds or just people in general
- lethargy
- losing motivation

The goal is to, first, recognize your own early warning signs in their infancy and, second, take action to stop their invasion; you may very well not have to get to the point where you actually *feel* depressed. What a great concept.

I'LL JUST PULL UP THE SHEETS

Breaking Tasks Down into Smaller Components

Sometimes the weather outside is lousy and the house is cold; sometimes it's sunny and bright and the day is full of reasons to get up and join the living. And then there are those days when it doesn't make a bit of difference what the weather is like because in bed and buried under the covers is the only place I want to be. I can almost hear the hypnotic voice of my bed wooing me. "Come to me. Stay with me. I'll keep you safe. I'll make that whole ugly thing of your so-called life disappear."

But it's only another lie that depression tries to suck me into with one goal in mind—to block out that tiny ray of sunshine called hope.

For anyone who's ever experienced a major or even not so major episode of depression, these words probably sound depressingly familiar. Crawling back into bed—or never getting out to begin with—in a feeble attempt to escape from life is perhaps the most classic picture of a depressed person. Or if you've ever lived with someone who was depressed, that lump under the covers can be an all too familiar sight.

But this isn't a chapter on how to escape. Instead, I want to share how I put a whole new spin on what it can mean to "just pull up the sheets."

Even the most basic, routine tasks—like making my bed—can seem overwhelming and can actually add to my overall feelings of fatigue, despair, and futility of life when I'm depressed. Depression and productivity are pretty much mutually exclusive.

But they don't have to be.

One of the best tools I've discovered for helping myself reenter life is to experience a sense of accomplishment. To actually do even one small task can have surprising results. By breaking down tasks into smaller parts, the possibility of experiencing a sense of accomplishment increases dramatically. And yes, even the simplest of tasks such as making my bed can be broken down into individual opportunities to accomplish something.

When making my bed seems like more than I can possibly manage, I can tell myself, "I'll just pull up the sheets…I can manage that." More often than not, and always to my utter amazement, once having pulled up the sheets, I actually feel encouraged—even energized—by the immediate sense of accomplishment of having done more than I thought I could. So I decide that I can pull up the blanket too. With that done, I discover that I can tackle the comforter as well. My sense of accomplishment steadily growing, I decide that putting the pillows in place was something I can manage as well. In a matter of minutes, I look at my very nicely made bed and enjoy the shocking realization that I had just accomplished more than I thought possible.

This one improbable accomplishment of making my bed has, on more than one occasion, brightened my outlook and built my confidence to the point of tackling something even more challenging…like getting dressed.

It really doesn't take long to get the hang of this whole idea of breaking down tasks into smaller components. And I'm confident that if I can do it even when I'm depressed, you can too.

Here are a few ideas to get you started:

If taking a ten-minute walk seems too daunting, try just walking to the end of the block, then reevaluating whether to continue on or head back home. If fixing something to eat is overwhelming in its magnitude, maybe getting a couple crackers out of their box in the cupboard is possible. With box in hand, you might find that you're able to open the refrigerator for some milk to go along with those crackers. Or what about the sink full of dishes from last week when you *were* able to fix a meal or two? Perhaps just setting the crusty pan to soak is a not-too-overwhelming concept, which in turn could lead to doing the silverware, which could lead to—I think you get the idea.

The point is that the reality of breaking down tasks that we don't think of as having parts is exactly that—a reality. Opportunities for discovering we can do more than we thought possible are everywhere, every day. They're simple, they're practical, and they're achievable.

Reality also says that there will be days when just pulling up the sheets and stopping is all I end up accomplishing. Even on those days, as I get myself off the sofa and crawl back into that partially made bed at the end of the day, I can remind myself that I actually accomplished something. Then as I drift off to sleep, I can allow myself the luxury of feeling good about that one small accomplishment.

So whether it's just pulling up the sheets or walking to the end of the block or rinsing a couple of dirty dishes, go ahead, and let yourself genuinely enjoy the sense of accomplishment. It's not childish, silly, demeaning, or pointless. It's important. The truth is that doing anything at all when you're depressed is reason to celebrate…reason for hope.

TELL ME WHERE IT HURTS

Getting Medical Help

In my head,
 In my throat,
  In my chest,
   In my bones,
    In my muscles,
     In my energy level,
      Everywhere and nowhere.

It feels like the flu,
 It feels like a heart attack,
  It feels like stress,
   It feels like PMS that doesn't stop,
    It feels like I'm being strangled.

So how's a person supposed to know when to get help?

The simplest answer is that if your symptoms (and there'll be more than one) have been nagging you for two weeks or more, it's time to get it checked out. It may or may not be clinical depression, but whatever it is, it should be checked out by a trusted health care provider.

But which one?

Once again, the simple answer is best. Start with your family doctor, primary care provider, internist, whatever label is given to the medical professional that oversees your general medical issues. If you don't have one, ask friends or relatives for recommendations. You don't have to go into the gory details of why you need a doctor; it's just a wise thing for all of us to have a personal doctor. If finances keep you from making an appointment, check into what local free or low-cost clinics there may be in your area. Swallow your pride, and do it.

Remember, you're worth taking care of.

So you've made the appointment. You're sitting in the waiting room feeling like everybody is staring at you. At least that's how it was for me when I finally took my symptoms seriously and went to the doctor.

When you're asked any of several times during this visit, "Why are we seeing you today?" be honest. This may feel like the challenge of the century because, if you're like me, you feel foolish trying to sound coherent in describing the smorgasbord of symptoms you've been dealing with. But I'll say it again, "Be honest."

The simple answer is once again often the most helpful: "I think I'm depressed."

There, you've said it.

If your doctor is on his or her toes, he/she will take you seriously and begin asking you to describe the symptoms that are causing you to think that. It's a legitimate question and not meant to patronize you or make light of your answer.

Being direct and admitting that you think you might be depressed is also a helpful way to potentially avoid unneeded, expensive tests. I know of a woman who went through test after test with no success trying to determine the cause of her symptoms. Ultimately, she went to the Mayo Clinic where she got an accurate diagnosis: panic disorder.

If your doctor wants to refer you to a psychiatrist, once again swallow your pride. Remind yourself that he has your health as his priority. He wants you to get the best help possible and that very well could be from a specialist.

I remember when my (new) doctor wanted to refer me to a psychiatrist, I was inwardly ticked off. We had just moved to a different state, and all I wanted was my prescription refilled. He wanted me to see a shrink. He said that he wasn't comfortable authorizing the prescription dosage I had been taking.

"Okay, fine, if that's the way it has to be, then I guess I've got no choice."

As it turns out, it was absolutely the best thing that could have happened. Once under the care of the specialist,

I began getting the help I needed, including the right meds. I am forever grateful that my new primary care doc *wasn't* comfortable and instead followed his medical instincts to send me to a specialist. And when it comes to clinical depression, the specialist is a psychiatrist.

So the following is the answer to "When should I get medical help?"

Well, if your symptoms have been significantly disrupting your life for two weeks or longer, now would be a great time to make that appointment.

ONE SIZE DOESN'T FIT ALL

Different People, Different Symptoms

This could actually be considered "Tell Me Where It Hurts, Part 2."

At some point in almost everyone's life, it will be helpful, if not essential, to have a basic understanding of how medical professionals determine whether a patient should be diagnosed with clinical depression.

Whether you are the person who seems depressed or you are living with, working with, or related to someone who appears to be depressed, it's a good idea to know what the distinguishing marks of depression are.

We are often aware of symptoms for many other medical conditions ranging from measles to heart attacks to

Alzheimer's. We know that if a person's skin looks yellow, there's a good chance something's gone awry with the liver. If someone's eyes seem to have a cloudy appearance, we are fairly sure that it's cataract. If a person quickly loses the color in their face, we may want to make sure someone is close by in case that person faints.

Obviously, I'm oversimplifying what it looks like to have any of these conditions, and I'm certainly not trying to make light of any of them. Each is a medical condition that needs intervention on some level.

And so it is with depression.

Regardless of age, station in life, education, or whatever, there are still so many of us that don't have a good understanding of what qualifies as a major depressive episode.

A major depressive episode or disorder is more than a lingering feeling of sadness or feeling blue or feeling being down in the dumps.

The most accurate way for me to help you understand— or to help you help others understand—what it officially is, is to let you know what the DSM-IV TR has to say about it. The DSM-IV TR is the most current diagnostic manual, but as I understand it, there will likely be a new edition somewhere in the foreseeable future. DSM stands for Diagnostic and Statistical Manual of Mental Disorders. The IV means that it's the fourth edition, and the TR means there's been a text revision.

There's been a part of me that has inwardly cringed and wanted to separate myself from the term mental disorder. The same goes for the term mental illness. Maybe you have that same reaction. By now in my journey, I've pretty much come to terms with the terms so to speak. On occasion, I still need to lightheartedly remind myself that depression involves the brain's ability or inability to appropriately process thoughts and emotions and/or other physiological responses. I use *appropriately* in the sense of the response being healthy and beneficial for my mind and body. The bottom line is that depression involves the brain's ability to process certain stimuli. Brain equals mental, so we are stuck with the terms mental illness and mental disorder. Note to self: Uh-duh.

Words can often reflect negative attitudes and biases. Unfortunately, that has been the history for mental illnesses. This has improved greatly since those first eight months on the sofa I told you about, and yet the stigma and misunderstandings persist. I've made it somewhat of a personal campaign to rattle people's cages and get them to see mental illness in a less looked down on way. I don't try to hide the fact that I have a mental illness called bipolar disorder (a.k.a. manic depression). When people learn that, I can get looks and even comments that say in effect, "You don't *look* crazy." And that's my goal—to tear down stereotypes. At sixty years old, I jokingly confess that I want to be the poster child for the National Mental Health Association.

Okay, time to get off my soapbox and back on the subject of the diagnostic criteria for clinical depression.

You could Google the term depression and, with lightning speed, have multiple links to the DSM-IV TR. You *could* do that, but let me just give you the essentials right here instead.

Important note from me: this isn't meant to be an exact duplication of the DSM but rather provide the essence and essentials of it. So here you go:

At least five of the following symptoms have been present during the same two-week period and represent a change from previous functioning. Plus, at least one of the symptoms is either number 1 or number 2.

1. Depressed mood most of the day, nearly every day.
2. Markedly diminished interest or pleasure in all, or almost all, activities most of the day, nearly every day.
3. Significant weight loss when not dieting or weight gain (significant means a change of more than 5 percent of body weight in a month), or decrease or increase in appetite nearly every day.
4. Insomnia or hypersomnia (sleeping too much) nearly every day.
5. Psychomotor agitation or retardation nearly every day that is observable by others, not merely subjective feelings of restlessness or being slowed down.
6. Fatigue or loss of energy nearly every day.

7. Feelings of worthlessness or excessive or inappropriate guilt (which may be delusional) nearly every day (this is more than self-reproach or guilt about being sick).

8. Diminished ability to think or concentrate, or indecisiveness, nearly every day.

9. Recurrent thoughts of death (not just fear of dying), recurrent suicidal ideation without a specific plan, or a suicide attempt or specific plan for committing suicide.

Additional considerations for diagnosis include:

- The symptoms cause clinically significant distress or impairment in social, occupational, or other important areas of functioning.

- The symptoms are not due to the direct physiological effects of a substance (for example: drug abuse or a medication side effect) or a general medical condition, such as hypothyroidism.

- The symptoms are not better accounted for by bereavement (after the loss of a loved one, for example) unless the bereavement symptoms persist for longer than two months or are characterized by marked functional impairment, morbid preoccupation with worthlessness, suicidal ideation, psychotic symptoms, or psychomotor retardation.

Hopefully, this gives you valuable insight and understanding of the range and variety of depression symptoms. As I mentioned briefly earlier, the symptoms don't necessarily present themselves in the same way from person to person and won't always be the same combination of symptoms from episode to episode even for the same person.

A word to the wise (that's you and me): don't get caught in the trap of self-diagnosis. The symptoms mentioned are meant to be a tool to help you know what depression looks like and to give you insight on when to seek professional help.

I JUST WANT TO BE NORMAL...WHATEVER THAT IS

Recognizing Healthy Responses to Negative Situations

So it's been several months since you were finally able to shake off that nasty little guy—depression. He'd had his claws firmly embedded into your scalp—no wait—you're entire body for quite a while. But now he's gone, and you've found your way back into the land of the living.

Of course, you're not kidding yourself; you know you need to stay up with your meds, your sleep routine, your exercise—all those good things you've been learning about your own symptom management. But you've been functional. Actually, better than functional. You feel normal.

Normal is good.

It's enjoyable to stay home because you choose to and not because you can't manage to leave.

It's fun to stay in your jammies once in a great while for reasons other than having no desire or energy to get dressed.

It's even kind of nice getting tears in your eyes watching a chick flick.

It's great to be able to go to the grocery store and not want to hide down the next aisle if you see someone you know.

It's downright great to laugh.

It's good to be able to focus enough to get your work done. Actually, going to work isn't that bad. And if that irritating coworker would decide to quit, that would make it even better. But for the time being, you can live with the situation, and that in itself feels good.

Normal is good. We like normal.

Then the unexpected comes. Something legitimately sad happens. It could be anything, big or little. It's something that would make a normal person sad.

So now what? Stuff the sadness because it feels a little like depression? Or there's that fleeting thought that if you let yourself feel sad, you'll spiral down to the pit again?

How well I remember those thoughts. I remember the feeling of fear that if I let myself feel anything that is not up, I'll end up going all the way down to the pit again. I even remember thinking, *How does a normal person do this?* We can't avoid sadness in this life, so what are we going to do when it comes along?

The absolute most important thing to remember—well, to learn first and then remember—is that we were created to experience emotions. God created emotions. God experiences emotions. And because Jesus took on human form, God can actually feel human emotions. That's amazing.

Anyway, back to my point. We were created to experience emotions. There is a normal, healthy, emotional reaction for each and every one of life's experiences.

Oh, by the way, from this point on in this chapter, when I say normal, I mean healthy, and by healthy, I mean in line with how we were created.

Knowing that, we can move on to allowing ourselves to react appropriately to the situation. Perhaps the key word to all this is "appropriately."

Just as it is appropriate to feel happy when you get an unexpected gift, a raise, or some good news, it is equally appropriate to feel sad when sad things happen.

Of course, this isn't limited to being sad. Sometimes, apprehension can be normal; sometimes, anger can be healthy. I believe that there can even be normal, healthy reasons for feeling depressed. Perhaps that's one reason for the term clinical depression as opposed to just depression. Whatever the emotion, there are healthy, as well as unhealthy, reasons for feeling how you do, just as there are healthy and unhealthy ways to express those feelings.

My advice? Let yourself feel.

In our journey of learning what it means to experience all of life—the good and the bad, the happy and the sad—there is a learning curve. But it's not as difficult as you might think. Plus there are lots of resources available (people, books, classes, support groups) where we can increase our understanding of what a healthy response looks like in various situations. This would be especially true with the deep sadness of grieving the loss of a significant part of your life, whether it's a person, a job, or whatever. Everyone grieves in their own way. Knowing that, if this happens to be the case for you, please check out a support group, counselor, pastor, or friend who can walk through this time with you.

For those of us who have the additional challenge of the tendency toward clinical depression, there is another aspect to be mindful of. That would be in staying aware of how far reaching that emotion is. Does your sadness have a focus? Can you say, "I'm sad because…" and have a specific something to fill in the blank? If you can't, then you'll probably want to watch out for other signs that your body chemistry is morphing in ways that could become clinical depression. Even if you don't see, or aren't aware of, any other signs, it would still be a good idea to look at your symptom management basics and see if something has begun to slide into nonuse. For example, has there been even a dose or two that you've missed in your medication routine? After being on my own medication regime for over fifteen years, I'm still amazed at how easy it is for me to forget either my morning or evening meds. If that happens more than once in a week, it's predictable that I will feel the effects of the missed doses three or four days later. By now, I've seen the correlation enough so that when it happens, I can just mentally weather out the day or two of feeling somewhat off-kilter.

One of the most common telltale signs that an emotion is fueling another trip into clinical depression is whether or not it is coloring all aspects of your daily life. Again, it's not uncommon for sadness from a significant loss to do this, which reinforces my previous suggestion for grief support.

As I'm writing this chapter, I've got a virus that has given me laryngitis, and I'm feeling like…you know…like I have a cold. I'm feeling draggy and tired. And yet, I was still able to do what I needed to do today, including working on this book. Had depression been the reason for feeling how I do, I very possibly would not have had the mental—or physical—oomph to get it done. I think there's a good lesson hidden in there. A cold can slow me down and the stomach flu can send me to bed, but depression can incapacitate me down to my very soul. I'm so glad I have a cold.

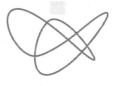

MY ENEMY, MY FRIEND

Embracing the Positive
Side of Depression

It always amazes me to realize that some of life's most profound lessons have come when I least expect them and didn't even know I was looking. Maybe that's the definition of epiphany.

I remember one of my life's epiphanies in particular. This particular one came during a routine visit with my doctor to monitor my meds. Yes, I do take meds, just in case you were wondering. But more on that subject later.

There was nothing particularly memorable about anything else at this appointment. Maybe that's why her comment stands out like it does. It was an incredibly sincere and downright enthusiastic remark—coming from a psychiatrist no less. She said, "Bipolar people are the coolest!"

I don't remember if I made any sort of intelligible comment in response. I was too busy picking my chin up off the floor. The appointment continued on as if nothing life changing had happened, but it had. It gave me a lot to think about on my drive back home and many times since then as well. Much to my own surprise, I've actually come to the place in my life where I agree with her. Amazing.

You see, up until that point, I hated the fact that I had this thing in my life that manages to affect every area of my life—negatively. For me, living with this disorder was as enjoyable as waltzing with a porcupine while simultaneously carrying a backpack full off rocks on my back and juggling multiple glasses of water, making it necessary for the porcupine to hold me closer in order to keep up with the music. Just describing it makes me exhausted.

Up until that memorable comment by my doctor, I viewed the symptoms of bipolar disorder to be my mortal enemy. I didn't see anything good about living with bouts of severe depression. Life was a ping-pong tournament of episodes of depression, followed by periods of normalcy, followed by depression, followed by another period of normalcy, followed by a period of depression. To keep things interesting, every once in a while, there would be periods of hypomania sprinkled in just for fun. The hypomanic times brought increased self-esteem and energy, but with it also came racing thoughts and speech, disrupted sleep patterns, and a trail of unfinished projects to stare at me when I came back to a place of more emotional stability. Why would I (or anyone) want to embrace something like that as a friend?

Over time, what my doctor helped me to see is that the same people who are susceptible to acute episodes of depression and bipolar disorder are also gifted with intelligence, insightfulness, and artistic abilities. So since I was so willing to identify with the negative sides of depression and mania, I needed to be open to acknowledging the positives as well. Someone with more education than I currently have could probably adequately explain why those who deal with depression are also generally gifted in those other areas, but when it comes right down to it, I really don't need to understand the biology and physiology of it to except the truth of it. I've always known that my level of intelligence is above average and that I've enjoyed playing the piano, violin, and cello along with other creative and artistic endeavors. Those were all things that I liked about myself, but I'd never considered the possibility that the same predisposition toward developing bipolar disorder was also the reason behind some of the best parts of me.

I discovered something else over the years since that original epiphany. If I had to give up the intelligence and talents I have been blessed with in order to eliminate the challenges of depression and mania in my life, I wouldn't do it. So it's true. Bipolar disorder is my *frenemy*.

So go ahead…take a look at the strengths and talents you have been blessed with. If you find yourself at a place where you're not able to see a single valuable thing in who you are, ask a caring friend or relative to help you because there is much more to you than you may realize. For me, that person was my sister. She wrote out this long list of all the positives she saw in me. It was actually hard to read the list. Knowing my sister wouldn't lie to me meant she was telling me the truth and that gave me permission to believe what she had written. I still have that list, and every once in a while, I take it out and reread it to remind myself of who I really am.

It doesn't matter if the depression you deal with is the bipolar flavor of depression. It doesn't matter if the actual symptoms look like mine or anybody else's. What does matter is recognizing that depression is not the whole picture of who you are. So as you stop to look inside, or listen to what someone you trust sees, be willing to believe in and embrace the good stuff that makes you who you are—the whole you, the one of a kind, fabulous person you were created to be.

LIVING "AS IF"

The Road Out

As if what?
As if I'm not depressed?
As if I have don't have zero motivation?
As if I don't care about anything anymore?
As if I don't want to talk to anyone?
As if I don't cry every day?
As if I feel rested?
As if… (You can fill in the blank.)

The answer is yes…sort of. Not exactly helpful is it? Let me try to explain.

I have found it a delicate balance between denial and a healthy "as if" approach to my day.

There's been many a time where I've sensed the early nibbles of depression and did nothing to try to stop the onset. Being aware of what my symptoms are but desperately wanting to *not* be depressed (again), I've tried to put blinders on. I've tried to tell myself that I'm really not experiencing what I think I'm experiencing. If I ignore it, whatever "it" is will just disappear.

I treat those first nibbles "as if" they don't signal the very real indication of the onset of another bout of depression for who knows how long or how dark.

When I choose this outlook, it invariably doesn't work. It has sometimes taken days for me to figure that out. Graciously, there have been times when the depression hasn't gotten a full foothold, and there's still time for self-intervention to avoid a deeper or lengthier period of depression.

However, if I'm going to be honest—and of course I am—times of ignoring those first signs have generally led to my not being able to prevent them from leading me into a deeper and longer time of depression.

Here's the reality:

To try and ignore—or even downplay—the importance of those first nibbles is to be in denial. Not surprisingly, I have found that denial is never the way to avoid or escape the authenticity of anything.

What the specific steps are that will help you prevent your first symptoms from escalating varies from person to person and can also vary from time to time. As you become familiar with what your particular early warning signs are, you will learn what strategies work best for the specific symptoms. My hope is that by the time you've read this little book, you'll have a better understanding of what those signs are for you and what you can do to reduce the risk of sliding down into that deep black pit.

In other words, when it comes to early warning signs, living "as if" means treating those first suspicious signs "as if" they are an opportunity to take steps to avoid depression's claws digging in deeper. Because, truthfully, that's exactly what they are.

The other aspect of living "as if" at this early stage is to take action "as if" you are not the victim. Act "as if" you're not the victim of depression, "as if" you're not the victim of your symptoms, and "as if" you're not helpless to do anything about it.

You can do much to determine what your next few days or weeks can be, and doing much is often really very little. Does that make sense? It's like getting a headache; the earlier you take a pain reliever, the faster and easier you will be able to reduce the symptoms. At the risk of repeating myself, "taking a pain reliever after the pain is full blown is like putting on an asbestos glove *after* you've put your hand into the fire."

It's remarkably similar with depression. The earlier the intervention, the more likely it is to experience the most benefit from your efforts. So I'll say it again: "You are not the victim." By acknowledging the early signs, you put yourself in a position to take charge of the progression of those beginning symptoms.

Oh, before I forget to mention it:

If you're not sure you're getting depressed but think you might be, in the words of my former psychiatrist, "You are." In other words, treat it "as if" you are. Act "as if" you are getting depressed, and take steps to prevent its invasion into your life.

Even after saying all that, I have to admit there have been times when I've not been able to prevent the downward slide. Sometimes depression has a mind of its own even in the early stages.

Why?

Who knows? Perhaps it's because I didn't acknowledge all the early signs. Perhaps it's because I wasn't as diligent as the symptoms required. Perhaps it's just because this time is different. It really doesn't matter why. It is what it is.

Because of that potential, I'm telling myself, as well as you, "Please don't let the possibility that your efforts might not be enough get in the way of doing all you can to avoid the development of major depression."

So what about those times when, for whatever reason, we're smack-dab in the middle of being depressed. There's no way of denying the fact that you are significantly depressed. You have all your predictably intrusive depression symptoms and even a different one thrown in the mix occasionally. Isn't that just great?

You don't want to get out of bed.

    You don't want to fix anything to eat.

        You don't want to get together with your friends.

            You don't want, you don't want, you don't want.

  Then what?

  Then, we take living "as if" to a different level.

Rise to the challenge. Make choices, and take action "as if" you *do* want to

    get out of bed,

        fix something simple to eat,

          get together with friends,

or perhaps you're sounding more like…

I can't call her.

    I can't go to church.

        I can't get dressed.

          I can't go to class.

          I can't pray.

            I can't eat.

              I can't, I can't, I can't…

Can you guess what my next suggestion will be? I bet you *can*.

Here it is: Rise to the challenge. Take action, even the tiniest, most unexciting actions, "as if" you *can*.

In either scenario, it's very possible that you will surprise yourself with unexpected activity. You may feel emotionally drained or physically pushed to your limit, but you will have actually done something you didn't think you could do.

It feels almost "as if," even for a moment, that you're not depressed. And that's a great step in the right direction. With each "as if" action, you will begin to see more and more light at the end of the tunnel.

And *that's* a great feeling.

IT'S NOT ABOUT PRAYING MORE

Keeping Religiosity Out of Recovery

As you may have already experienced, one of the most counterproductive attempts at helpful suggestions that can be inflicted on someone under the dark cloud of depression goes something like this: "If you only had more faith (prayed more, believed more, etc.), the depression would be gone."

This is a tricky one, and I realize I may be venturing out onto sensitive ground, but here goes.

I had the opportunity to facilitate a depression recovery support group for three years. During those three years, over two hundred people attended the depression recovery group for varying lengths of time. Of those, 98–99 percent were church-going, faith-oriented, real people who loved God.

How can that be?

For now at least, the "how" isn't important. More important is the fact that Christians are not immune to experiencing significant bouts of major depression. And all too often, it can be seen as a dark personal shame meant to be hidden or discounted—even from ourselves.

As followers of Christ, we live by faith in a loving God who *can* heal and *does* heal and has paid the necessary price for us to experience healing—spiritual, physical, emotional, and yes, mental. Scriptures, and untold numbers of confirming experiences down through the ages, give us valid and rational reason to be certain of this.

And yet, the reality of depression within the body of Christ and community of faith cannot be denied or ignored. Unfortunately, in many well-intended attempts to help others experience healing and freedom from depression, the outcome is often counterproductive (read: hurtful).

There are most certainly times and situations where a spirit of depression needs to be sent packing through the effective prayer of any and all who, through the death and resurrection of Jesus Christ, have been given authority to speak in his name.

There are also times—as in my own story—where miraculous healing of a biochemical imbalance or neurotransmitter malfunction can be experienced as a result of prayer.

However, to communicate with someone (including yourself) who is experiencing depression by assuming, judging, or otherwise implying it to be evidence of either a lack of diligent prayer or insufficient faith is just plain wrong. (Ouch!)

Being on the receiving end of a matter-of-fact determination that your ongoing struggle is due to a lack of faith, unconfessed sin, or a work of the enemy is not helpful, or even kind. In my own experience, even the most sincerely compassionate of such efforts ends up (at least temporarily) mentally and emotionally reinforcing the pervading depression-induced self-condemnation and hopelessness.

However (and here's the challenge), there are times and situations when depression *is* a spiritually based condition that must be dealt with as such. My strong encouragement to those who have accurately discerned this is to pray before you speak; sometimes, that's all you're meant to do. Speak only if you must and then only when it has the best potential of being received.

There are also times, regardless of the specific disease, disorder or condition, miraculous healing is precisely what God is doing in that person's life at that moment...not too different than when Jesus healed only one man, out of the many, at the Pool of Bethsaida. To be present in those times is to be on holy ground.

But for all those times when we are on the receiving end of misguided suggestions for helping—either subtle or blatant—how can we appropriately respond, especially when God seems (and I stress "seems") so incredibly remote and inaccessible?

I really don't have any humorous anecdotes to help express any pearls of wisdom, but from a heart that has been where you are and seen both sides, let me say this:

You are loved and accepted just as you are. He is not judging you, condemning you, or giving up on you. His ways are filled with compassion and mercy even when you can't feel it, see it, or barely even believe it. He knows where you're at and loves you just the same as when you are your best, undepressed self. He knows what is at the root of the depression you're experiencing, be it physical, mental, emotional, or spiritual, and he knows how to lead you back into where you can see and feel the "Son-shine."

You are his beloved child, and he consistently, unceasingly, perfectly loves you and sees your immense value.

Now, give yourself permission to believe it...because it's true.

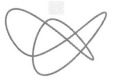

EARLY TO BED, EARLY TO RISE

Setting My Personal Biological Clock

It's continually amazing to me that managing depression symptoms affects so many areas of daily life. That could potentially sound overwhelming, but in reality, it's actually more encouraging than overwhelming.

It not only gives each of us a much larger picture of how depression affects our lives but also many more opportunities to manage our experience of depression, including...

Sleep, wonderful sleep.

Sleep is often a huge challenge when we're depressed. We either sleep too little or too much. Often, it is an unrelenting mixture of both. We sleep too little and end up dragging ourselves through each new day. We sleep too much, so when we finally get out from under the covers, we end up dragging ourselves through the day. *Hmm*...there seems to be a pattern here. Did you notice it? However, it's not a pattern that has any positive benefit for anyone...especially for those of us carrying the weight of depression on our tired and weary shoulders.

In my humble and nonprofessional opinion, *irregular* sleep patterns are greatly responsible for how we function—physically, mentally, and emotionally. It's not just that we sleep too much or too little. However, I'm not giving you permission to indulge your pattern of choice. I have found that the problem lies in the combination of too little and too much. Over the course of time—and it doesn't necessarily take very many days (or nights) to be "over the course of time"—an irregular sleep pattern develops and exacerbates (I love that word.) our other depression symptoms.

That's all well and good to know, but how do we capture those z's? Or how do we shake off the lethargy when those same z's hypnotize us into a drug-like state of mind and body in the mornings?

The self-help answers are surprisingly simple and straightforward. But please remember that if your sleep-related challenges are significant enough to not respond to my suggestions—or your own—check in with your doctor. He or she needs to know this.

With that being said, if you're sleeping too little because you don't feel sleepy, go to bed anyway. Put yourself in the position (literally and figuratively) to invite sleep to come. Perhaps a warm bath beforehand will help. Or perhaps a cup of chamomile tea will help do the trick.

Once in bed, if you're having trouble falling to sleep, you can try things like listening to soothing music or reading a not-too-fascinating book. A personal favorite is attempting to do mathematical calculations in my head. I know it's weird, but it works.

As a born-again Christian, I highly recommend prayer. Take these times as opportunities to speak words of love, thankfulness, and gratitude to God. I earnestly encourage you to keep these times free from asking for this and for that but rather filled with praise and worship. Generally speaking, prayer *as an activity to encourage sleep* is more successful if your prayer focus is not on your or others' needs and hurts. If finding the words to pray without asking for anything is beyond your ability in those times, try reading from the Psalms where there are hundreds of words of comfort, praise, and worshipful faith to be found.

And if you're sleeping too much, get up even though you don't want to. I can't think of any other more enticing way to say it. Sorry. Thankfully, you're not without some strategies that can help. If you work a day job or have children at home (oh, wait, that *is* a day job), you have built in motivation. If you don't have either of those routine commitments, try to create some personally motivating strategies. It might help to schedule any hair appointments, doctor appointments, etc., for midmorning. It can even be an appointment to meet a friend at Starbucks. Midmorning appointments have proven to be realistic enough for me to manage. Even if I get my day started a little later than what would be ideal, at least I'm up and productive, which helps me to actually be more likely to be able to fall asleep at the end of the day.

Creating strategies to help you not sleep your day away is also an area where others that care about you can help in a very practical way. If they don't already know, tell them you're struggling with getting up and going. Ask them to call you at a predetermined time or even come over to obnoxiously and repeatedly ring your doorbell. Well, not too obnoxiously or repeatedly; you don't want to start your day both groggy *and* grumpy.

There is another culprit when it comes to problems with sleep. It's one that tends to derail my attempts more often than I'd like to admit. There's really no warm and fuzzy way to say it—the culprit is…lack of discipline.

If you're like me, the end of the day is when self-discipline is most needed. Mornings seem to have several built-in or simple-to-incorporate motivators as I've mentioned briefly already.

Whatever the reason behind your particular challenges, here are a few basic ideas for improving your sleep pattern:

First, however you can, determine what your own realistic and normal sleep needs are, which will most likely be somewhere between seven and a half to nine hours a night. Then, consider your typical daily activities in order to determine what *your* getting up and going to bed goals should be. Not everybody's life is 9–5, so it's a lesson in frustration trying to put a square peg in a round hole so to speak. Even if each day is not identical, treat them in such a way as to help facilitate a *regular* sleep pattern. Doing this has the added benefit of helping to see why you're not getting the rest you need.

It can be amazing to realize how much discipline it takes to turn off the TV, step away from the computer, and turn off the cell phone. Make sure there's a way for you to be contacted in an emergency, but please…no sending or receiving texts during your sleep hours. Those hours are sacred.

You might have other activities that keep you up. Even what you eat and how late in the day you eat or when you exercise can impact your ability to get to sleep and have a good night's sleep. Whatever those things are for you, you can adjust those activities to give you the best chance for a good night's sleep. It's also important to allow time for your nighttime routines and the typical amount of time it takes you to fall asleep once you're in bed. Remember, the goal is to get a certain amount of actual sleep time.

The more you learn to provide yourself with a regular sleep pattern, the less chance that sleep issues will worsen any depression symptoms. Healthy, regular sleep is good medicine…and it's free. Do I hear a woo-hoo?

HELLO, MY NAME IS...

Surviving Social Situations

Most definitely, when we're depressed, the key word here is "surviving." I'm not even talking about more complex responses like enjoying. Just surviving is what it's about.

Social situations can take on many forms. It's more than going to your cousin's wedding or being a greeter at church. Social situations include answering the phone, going through the checkout line at the grocery store, and going to work. A social situation is anything that involves at least one other person.

Have you noticed how often expressing ourselves—to ourselves or to others—is accompanied by "n't" when we're depressed?

I can't, I don't, I shouldn't, I didn't, I won't, and on and on.

This can be abundantly evident just anticipating social situations.

"I can't face them right now. I'm just not up to it."

"I don't think I can answer the phone. I'll just let it go to voice mail."

"I shouldn't feel this way about going to church, but I just can't deal with being around people today."

"I didn't know I would have to stay through the whole meeting. If I'd known that, I would've called in sick."

"I won't go to dinner with them. I'm not a very good company today."

Actually, when we sift it all down to one "n't," it would be *can't*. All those other "n'ts" are simply rewording the underlining belief of "I can't."

So when it comes to surviving the *anticipation* of social situations, the key is to choose (and put to use) a different verb form.

"I *can* survive this."

Choosing this approach doesn't mean doing whatever "it" is for extended periods of time. Often the key to surviving the actual social situation is to give yourself permission to keep "it" short.

Perhaps going to the grocery store for just the one item you really need, then go to the self-checkout lane—or at least get in the shortest line. Actually, this is something both you and I probably already do. When we're not depressed, it's called efficient time management. Well, nothing's wrong with that concept even when we are depressed.

Or perhaps accepting an invitation to go out to dinner with friends can include explaining that you've had a long day and will need to make it an early evening.

Then there are those times when we've previously accepted an invitation to an event of some sort. (What *were* we thinking?) Anyway, the invitation has been accepted, and now the day's arrived. So take a shower, put on one of your favorite outfits (assuming it's appropriate for the occasion), and of course, your best smile. Sometimes it helps to give yourself a time frame. Perhaps you can stay just long enough to check out the dessert table and say thank you to the host. Or perhaps allow yourself to leave after you've been there for twenty-five minutes (That's so-o-o much shorter than a half hour, don't you think?).

The single most valuable survival tool is this: Get your focus off yourself and on someone else.

Is there somebody else that's looking left out? Be their friend.

Are you stuck in a one-on-one situation with someone you barely know? Get them talking about themselves.

Are there children at the event? Interact with them.

Is there something you can do to help? There are many times when extra help in the relative seclusion of the kitchen is greatly appreciated.

Even circulating with a plate of hors d'oeuvres can do the trick; most people will be more interested in looking at the food than at you. (Nothing personal; it's just natural.)

The essential ingredient is to do something for someone else—be others-focused, not self-focused.

The key attitude to hang on to is:

"You can do it."

And who knows, it's quite possible that you'll actually enjoy yourself. But even if you don't, you've done the right thing and the healthy thing, and that, my friend, is at least one big step beyond just surviving.

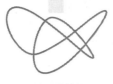

9 TO 5

The Impact of Holding a Job

As I sit here trying to decide how to tackle this subject, many thoughts cross my mind...

blue-collar jobs,
    white-collar jobs,
        self-employed,
            working full time,
                working part-time,
                    commission-only jobs,

being an at-home mom,
    being a single mom,
        being single,
       being married,
           needing to work but not able to,
             not needing to work but wanting to,
                    and on and on it goes.

Every work situation has its own set of considerations, its own set of advantages and disadvantages. Yet they all have one thing in common—being depressed negatively impacts our ability to work.

Even on the days when we make it to work, we may not be able to focus or to connect the dots for the simplest of our tasks. Maybe the day is going well; then an unexpected deadline comes up, and you fall to pieces. Maybe the anxiety of just being out of the house causes significant physical symptoms that you know are connected to being clinically depressed.

Realistically, there are probably as many different ways to approach these issues as there are different jobs, different people, and different schedules.

There is no magic pill to take, no obvious solution, but there *are* options.

First of all, is it essential that you work? (i.e. earn an income to pay the rent, to buy food, and to meet the minimum of life's necessities)

Most of us will be likely to answer, "Uh-duh…yeah."

But even if the answer is no, you probably have activities and responsibilities and commitments, for pay or not, that you want to be able to fulfill.

So if your daily activities and work life are being compromised by depression, take a quick inventory:

- If you are taking medication, are you being consistent and compliant with the dosage and frequency?
- Are you making your best effort to get enough sleep?
- Have you been eating right?
- Have you been getting outside at least a few minutes each day?
- Essentially, have you done all that you know will help?

If you recognize an area that has been even slightly neglected, it can have a bigger impact than you might be willing to acknowledge, but please do. Playing the ostrich role and sticking your head in the sand doesn't help. (Of course, you probably already know that, but I thought I'd mention it anyway.)

Get yourself back on track, remembering that it's going to take a day or two at the very least for your emotional stability to return. In the meantime, as much as possible, excuse yourself from as much of your routine responsibilities as you possibly can.

Do you have a friend or relative that can watch your kids overnight?

Can you not check your e-mail for a day or two?

Do you have any sick days or vacation leave that you can use?

And by all means, say no to anything that would interfere with getting yourself back on track.

But what if you've been doing your best with meds, sleep, diet, etcetera?

Have you been gradually (or not so gradually) getting involved in too many optional activities?

Sometimes when we're feeling good, feeling normal and functional, we allow ourselves to push the limits of healthy boundaries for our schedules and commitments.

Have you discussed your health issues with your boss or supervisor? Remember, depression is a health issue, one that does not need to be apologized for. I've known of people who have been able to work out arrangements that have made it possible for the employer's needs to be met and still give the employee the flexibility, the breaks, and the environment that make it possible to maintain a work life and be productive.

Oh, and one more question to ask yourself is whether you have made it a point to do at least one "because I want to activity" each day. Of course, I'm only talking about healthy, positive, self-nurturing activities. In addition to all those "I need tos" or "but they're counting on me tos" or the dreaded "shoulds," we need to leave room for the "want tos." It can be as simple as "I want to take a bath." (Then of course, take one, with bubbles preferably.)

It's been my experience that something as simple as taking time to play the piano or read a novel or bake some cookies is "good medicine."

Let me try to put it another way.

If you're like me, you probably tend to be a very responsible person when you're not depressed and/or you are a creative person in some capacity. Both of these traits are commendable. Yet if we feed one too much (the shoulds) and don't feed the other enough (the want tos), we're setting ourselves up for burnout. Burnout and depression are best friends.

For many people who live with depression, there are practical and successful strategies to maintain your work life.

For other people—including me—it hasn't been possible.

In 2001, I accepted a good-paying, temporary, five-month-long assignment with the State of Oregon. The position was challenging, which is generally a good thing for me, and there was the realistic potential that the position would become permanent.

Long story short, I crashed and burned. I couldn't even fulfill the five-month commitment. It was an extremely humbling (read: humiliating) experience, but one that made it impossible for me to ignore my limitations. I found out after the fact that those of us with bipolar disorder have a particularly difficult time maintaining regular employment. As my psychiatrist once told me, 80 percent of her patients with bipolar disorder have struggles with working; the other 20 percent aren't employed. I resigned from the position and began the two-and-a-half-year process of applying for, and ultimately receiving, Social Security disability benefits.

It's not a pretty story. I had to file bankruptcy, had my car repossessed, and sold my house. But in retrospect, it was worth the pain.

I discovered more about myself by *not* being able to work than I ever had in any of my various jobs over the years. I discovered a greater understanding of my creative nature, the importance of flexibility in my day-to-day routines, the impact of small stresses that build up over time, and so much more.

Above all, I discovered on a much deeper level the faithfulness, sovereignty, love, and mercy of God.

This seems like the perfect opportunity to say that trusting in Christ and choosing to let him be Lord is the one true reason for hope. The Bible contains many, many promises of provision, of rescue, of restoration, of sacred meaning behind it all for those who put their trust in Christ.

It's been over a decade since I was compelled to quit work. In the years since then, I've found increasing stability, love, and purpose beyond what I could have ever imagined for myself. At this point, I'm just over halfway to a bachelor's degree in psychology; then, God-willing, it's on to a masters in Christian counseling and a flexible, fulfilling work life for many more years after that.

Your story will be different than mine; it may have similarities, it may not. What is certain is that, in your work life, as with every other part of your life, God can and will make beauty from ashes.

I DIDN'T ASK TO BE BORN

Anger Turned Inward

Can you hear the sarcasm? Can you hear the frustration? Can you hear your own voice? (Ouch!)

Can you think of anybody who *did* ask to be born? Silly question, I know. So that should give us some kind of clue to something. But to what?

Well, let's see if we can figure that one out together.

If you're angry—even just inwardly—does that mean you're depressed?

Maybe yes, maybe no.

Can it lead to depression? Maybe yes, maybe no.

If you're depressed, does that mean you are angry? Maybe yes, maybe no.

If anger turned inward is somehow connected to depression, is it a cause or a symptom? Good question. (Aren't you glad this is such a helpful little book?)

There are many who agree that anger turned inward does describe depression. In fact, it was good ol' Sigmund Freud who originally used the anger tuned inward perspective, and his perspective continues to have wide acceptance. There are also those who don't agree and point out that anger is not mentioned in the DSM-IV's official diagnostic criteria for depression.

Personally, I'm of the opinion that whether or not anger is a cause or a symptom, it can certainly play a role in our experience of depression. I also don't believe the cause of depression is any singular component. And remember, I'm *not* saying any of this as some sort of professional expert but based on my own experience and the experiences of others that I've known.

Even if anger doesn't seem to be connected to your experience of depression, taking a look at anger to discover its cause and/or impact on our lives is a really good idea. However, for the sake of this chapter, I'm going to discuss anger in the context of it having a role in depression.

It certainly has had a role in my own experience.

In the chapter dealing with self-nurturing ("Down Time versus Feeling Down"), I'm going to be sharing some of what my struggles have been with believing I had any worth at all. My underlying (mis-) perception was that I was never meant to be born, so I certainly didn't *ask* to be born. If you want to take a break and read it now, go right ahead. I'll still be right here.

Okay, where was I? Oh, yeah, me not asking to be born.

One of the most common reasons for anger being turned inward is in response to failing to live up to our own set of excessively rigid or high standards. When you add up perceived failure after perceived failure, it's enough to make a person very inwardly angry.

That's exactly what it did with me.

Now, I didn't look like an angry person, and for the most part, I don't think others saw me as an angry person, but I was. I was angry at my infuriating inability to live up to my own standards. No matter how hard I tried, I kept failing to achieve my standards for personal perfection or, at the very least, acceptability.

As illogical as it sounds, ultimately, my response to my own failures was to try to help everyone else live up to my standards. I actually remember thinking, *If I can't get my own life right, then I'm gonna see that you get yours right.* How unkind. How ridiculous. How hurtful to relationships.

I can't say for certain, but as I'm writing this, I'm wondering that if the point in my life where I began to stop demanding perfection from others is the same point where personal failure and the anger I felt about it was the beginning of my own depression-related inner anger.

Hmm…interesting thought that had never occurred to me till just now. But I digress.

An equally harmful and potentially depression-inducing form of anger is the inability—or refusal—to express anger. Even a legitimate, hurt-prompted anger can often be turned inward by taking the blame for someone else's hurtful behavior. You don't get angry at the person; you don't even go home and kick the dog. You blame yourself and turn the anger inward.

Here's another possibility for how you might respond to something that has potential to make you angry: "It doesn't do any good to get angry." Sounds familiar? It does to me.

It almost sounds noble…almost.

In reality, it can be a mental rationalizing for the seeming uselessness of getting angry. It's a "why bother" reaction. The end result: the anger is not dealt with but rather gets buried in a dark corner of your inner self-labeled helpless and hopeless. It's in there that it can become fuel for depression.

So what's the secret for breaking away from the unhealthy ways we experience anger? How can we manage our depression symptoms by managing our anger?

For me, it has been a two-pronged effort.

The foundation for change has been an increasing trust in God's character, his sovereignty, and his intentions toward me. There are many different ways to accomplish this. Faith and choice are the starting place. From there, you and I can discover more of his character through his Word. By the way, if you don't have one already, try to find a Bible translation that makes it easy for you to understand, and that's usually *not* King James. I've also included a bunch of my favorite Bible verses in the "Additional Help" section.

Focused prayer and meditation on the truth of Scripture inwardly reinforces what we know to be true. Speaking those same truths out loud lets our ears hear what our hearts and minds believe. Writing out the verses that have been especially meaningful and helpful gets our eyes and bodies involved too. The more of our senses we use, the more firmly the truth can settle in and be at home in us.

The second prong has been, and continues to be, utilizing the strategies I've learned for breaking distorted thinking patterns. I'll be talking more about that later in the chapter titled "Going Out of My Mind." For now, I'll just say that you might want to read that chapter more than once because I can't express too strongly the positive impact that changing our patterns of thinking has on lessening—even eliminating—depression.

By now, you may be realizing that living life with anger turned inward is a lot more likely than you might have originally thought. The good news is that we don't have to be anger's victim.

And that makes one less thing to deal with on our journey.

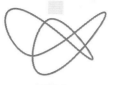

DOWN TIME VERSUS FEELING DOWN

The Importance of Self-Nurturing

I remember one particular morning of no importance. It wasn't long after I had recovered from an episode of major depression.

I remember staying at home, just kind of hanging out, doing not much of anything. I was totally enjoying my day. I remember being struck by how different it was to stay home without depression being the reason. I was staying home, probably still in my jammies, because I *chose* to be and not because I was depressed.

What a difference. What a revelation.

It was then that I began to realize the importance of self-nurturing.

If you're anything like me, the concept of being good to yourself can feel rather awkward…even wrong. Because we're so used to feeling bad about ourselves (not an uncommon condition for those of us who deal with depression), we become resistant or even out and out opposed to doing nice things for ourselves. Especially during those times when our entire being feels like one big dark hole, it's easy to believe that we don't deserve to be treated well by ourselves or anyone else.

What a lie.

For every person who spends any amount of time in the trap of self-hate, low self-esteem, self-doubt, or any other name you want to give to it, I would love to sit down with you and explain how valuable you are. I don't need to know you personally to know how valuable you are. I may not know what your valuable-ness looks like, but that doesn't change the fact that you have immense and eternal value. Your value isn't because of your abilities or your looks or your performance or anything else other than that you are *you*.

I'd like to share some of the long journey to become convinced of my own value.

From birth, without ever being told, without ever sensing a lack of love, I lived with the unspoken belief that I was a mistake. My birth was a mistake; my very existence was not meant to have happened. Even before I learned of some of the circumstances that may have given me some pseudo-rationale for that opinion, my very being was convinced of the truth of my belief.

As the years came and went, I realized how essential it was for me to behave in ways that would convince others it was okay for me to be alive. In my subconscious rationalization, my performance, my looks, and my choice of activities would cause others to accept that I was here on planet earth.

In essence, I was saying, "I may not deserve to be loved and nurtured, but at least, I can be acceptable...if I keep up the act."

Long story short, it wasn't until I was in my mid-thirties that I understood how wrong I was. In one brief sentence, a woman whose story was similar to mine said, "People decide when to make love. God decides when to make life."

Bam! It hit me like a lightning bolt. I was God's idea... always was, from *before* the beginning.

As more years went by and more mistakes and sorrows were experienced, I began to wonder how disappointed God must have been in what he had made...perhaps even regretting it.

Time for another lightning bolt.

This time, it came in the form of a mental picture. God was looking at me but kind of stepping back at the same time. Then I realized he wasn't trying to distance himself from me; he was admiring his handiwork and being very pleased. Wow.

So why am I telling you all that?

Because even though the circumstances may be different, the bottom line is the same: you are God's idea. He's pleased with you, his creation. It may sound a little corny, but God doesn't make junk, only priceless and unique beings to love and be loved by. If you're not already convinced of that truth, take some time to let it sink in.

Does it seem that I've gotten a little off track? I haven't really. I promise.

Self-nurturing is essential to promoting and enhancing our overall quality of life. The additional benefit is that it can act as a buffer from the self-loathing that often comes with depression.

Self-nurturing doesn't equal self-indulgence. Self-nurturing is treating yourself with value; it's taking care of yourself in a way that enhances your mental, physical, social, and spiritual well-being. However, if you don't start with an awareness of your personal worth, then any self-nurturing is defeated before you start.

So what does self-nurturing look like? The possibilities are limitless. Here are some of my personal favorites:

- When I have a long day in the "big city" (I live in rural northern Nevada so the big city is Reno), I make every effort to use the next day to recover. I avoid commitments, appointments, and schedules if at all possible.
- Since I live an hour and a half from the closest Starbucks, I treat myself to a mocha (Grande Mocha, two pumps, nonfat, no whip) when I do go to the big city. If at all possible, I drink it there so I can bring in

a book, read the paper, plan the rest of my day, or just enjoy a scone with my mocha.

- I don't overcommit. This one takes practice, but years ago, I found a great motivator. If I realize after the fact but before the event that I've overcommitted, I call and explain that I'm not able to do whatever it is after all. I find this so unpleasant that it really helps me be realistic about what I can commit to.
- I read a novel.
- I play the piano.
- I have lunch with a friend.
- I get out my special paper and pencil and draw.
- I try to keep an eye on what I eat but also allow myself an indulgence on occasion. "It's an event, not a lifestyle" is my motto for those times. I just need to make sure there's not too many events in a row.
- I take care of the basics like teeth, shower, hair, meals, exercise, and sleep. We all know that these are the things that are so very easy to neglect during periods of depression, so it's very self-nurturing to *not* neglect them.
- I try to always include at least one "want to" in each day along with all the "need tos."
- I've even been known to give myself a little present that I've gift-wrapped and saved for a time by myself…like when I'm at Starbucks.

- I've learned to accept compliments with just a sincere thank you.
- I make a point to finish a project I've been putting off. The feeling is awesome.

Perhaps most importantly, I've learned to acknowledge and appreciate my good qualities rather than throw them out with the trash.

So now that you've gotten some fresh insights about the importance of self-nurturing, go ahead…nurture yourself.

You deserve it.

PRIDE AND PREJUDICE

Being Receptive to Meds

It's a rare person indeed who experiences an extended bout of depression that is able to dig their way out of the black hole without the help of medication. So, of course, the earlier we can acknowledge that depression is creeping into our daily lives, the more chance there is to use other tools successfully and stop the advancing symptoms without meds.

But what if, for whatever reason, you're already there, and it's too dark and too much work to even think about trying to get back to the life you were meant to be living?

Or what if you're someone, like me, who has bipolar disorder where it has become necessary to need medication for extended periods or as a lifelong reality?

Or what if you're just now realizing that most of your life has been spent with a dark cloud hovering over your head, and you didn't even realize it?

Or what if someone you love dies—either expectedly or unexpectedly—and life refuses to give you any reason to think the grief will ever stop choking the life out of you?

What if your attempts using other self-help strategies haven't worked?

Then what?

Let me try to answer by starting with one more question.

Did you know that there are only two types of people in the world? (Slight pause.)

Those who think there are only two types of people and those who don't.

Sorry, I just couldn't resist sharing one of my favorite "punny" jokes. I don't know why, but I get a chuckle out of that one every time.

Seriously, though, when it comes to depression and its treatment, there are two types of people—those who are receptive to taking meds and those who aren't. I fell into the "those who aren't" category.

Back in the early nineties when I was first presented with the concept of taking meds to help alleviate my depression, I refused to even consider it. In my very illogical reasoning, taking meds was synonymous with admitting I was crazy. And of course, I wasn't, so why would I take meds?

As I shared with you in telling my own story in brief, I experienced a miraculous recovery from my first episode of major depression. It's my belief that, in God's mercy, he graciously stepped in that first time to give me time to learn more about what antidepressants are…and aren't.

It may be hard to imagine, but back then, just barely twenty years ago, Prozac was not a household word and drug advertising on TV was not even close to what it is today.

During that year between my first and second major episodes of depression, I found myself being exposed to a more realistic understanding of the role and value of antidepressants. Most significant was that, during this time, one of my brothers came for a visit, and I learned he had been diagnosed with bipolar disorder. It was largely through his knowledge and experience that I came to be receptive to the idea for my own life.

I have discovered over the years that one of my major misperceptions about antidepressants is shared by many, many others. The error is in thinking that there's a risk of becoming addicted. There is no more risk of that than there is of a diabetic becoming addicted to insulin. The blessing of medication, when properly prescribed, taken, and monitored, is that they assist the body (in this case, the brain) to function more as it was intended.

Very simply put, with clinical depression, the brain's neurotransmitters and synapses don't function as they are meant to. The right medication in the right dose assists the brain in its ability to have its neurotransmitters and synapses do their job better. There's so much more to the physiological processes that are involved, but hopefully, this gives you at least a little more insight in understanding. Although depression happens in your brain, the symptoms you experience are not just in your head…they're real, and they have a biological and physiological component that can often be helped with medication.

I have to admit that perhaps the pendulum has swung too far the other direction. With so much advertising and the abundance of medication choices, it's quite possible that there are many people taking antidepressants who don't fully understand that meds are only part of the answer…and sometimes *not* the answer when other strategies could be sufficient. This very fact is one of the main reasons I felt so strongly about writing this book. It's an important decision, one that needs to be made with the help and advice of your doctor and/or counselor.

So where do you see yourself on the subject? Do you fear becoming addicted to antidepressants? Do you see them as just a crutch? Or do you expect too much of them, thinking that a pill a day should wash all your troubles away?

My hope is that, after learning about this, you'll be open to meds while still recognizing that it's only one of the many tools we have available to us. If meds are appropriate for you like they are for me, we get the best benefit when we combine it with the other things we're doing to manage our symptoms.

And above all, always heed your doctor's advice and instructions when it comes to how and when to go on and off *any* medication.

There are some people, like myself, who will be best helped by keeping meds as an ongoing tool in our symptom management arsenal. Over the years, I have made a few attempts to test the waters by backing off on my meds. It's never worked, so I'm choosing to remain thankful that I have the option of medication rather than begrudge the fact that I need them.

There are also many, many others who can be helped by taking meds for a period of time, then not need to continue with them.

If your depression stems primarily from a bad situation, reaction to a traumatic event, illness, grief, loss, or any other of the numerous valid reasons that can exist, it's a realistic possibility that your need for antidepressants will fade as the other issues are resolved.

Another tangible reason for being open to meds is that sometimes we need to get ourselves back to emotional ground level in order to have the energy, motivation, and hopefulness needed to move past those circumstances.

Something else I've discovered through trial and error is that it is essential to entrust your medication needs to a doctor who is well trained in mental health issues and their treatment. Many well-intentioned, competent doctors are not specialized to the degree that you might need in order for you to achieve your highest level of mental and emotional health.

When I moved from Washington to Oregon, I absolutely hated it when my new primary care doc referred me to a psychiatrist. But in the end, it was the most amazingly right decision for him to have made. I discovered that I had been initially misdiagnosed by my previous primary care doctor. Turns out there are very different antidepressant choices for people who have bipolar depression versus other forms of clinical depression. Once properly diagnosed, my road to recovery made rapid improvement.

One last word of encouragement before we move on...

Please don't despair and give up if it takes some time to find the right medication for you, the right combination of meds, and/or the right dosage. I know from experience that it can be a scary thing to have to adjust and readjust. With every change, there is the time of transition and fine-tuning.

But hang in there.

It will be worth it in the end.

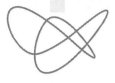

GOING OUT OF MY MIND

Breaking Distorted Thinking Patterns

Have you ever stopped to think about all the different ways that people describe "going out of my mind"? Me neither. Well, not until I started paying attention, that is.

It's kind of like never noticing how many red cars there are until you buy one. Then you see them everywhere.

Not fully taking into consideration the actual meaning of their words, it's common to hear people say things like "You're driving me crazy" or "I'm gonna lose my mind if I hear that song one more time" or these:

"He's bonkers."
    "She's nuts."
        "She's got a screw loose."

"They're all just crazy."
"He's losing his mind."

No matter how you say it, it's just another way of saying that you, or someone else, is crazy, and that's just another way to say insane, and insane is saying that you, or they, are not able to function in the real world because of severe mental defect.

I would guess that the vast majority of the times, comments like these are ways of expressing sarcasm, frustration, anger, or even attempts at humor. That doesn't make it right. In fact, it's my opinion that it is never helpful and often times hurtful. I believe that those types of comments and attitudes actually lessen compassionate understanding of what can be a very tragic condition for some…and that in itself is tragic.

But what about the times when we, during seasons of depression, absolutely believe we are indeed going out of our minds?

I know from much experience that there can be times where any or all those descriptions feel absolutely true. For me, it's often when there is too much action and interaction (in other words, noise) going on around me. In times past, it's been a hormonally triggered inability to cope with the normal daily routines, relationships, deadlines, or even the weather (yep, PMS). To be even more honest, sometimes it's been the result of words intentionally and hurtfully communicated by someone I cared about. When I combined those words with my own insecurities, I began to believe them.

However, this isn't going to be a chapter talking about all the different ways to be—or feel—crazy.

On the contrary, my friend.

The chapter title could perhaps be "Getting Back into My Mind," but I don't know…it just doesn't have the same ring to it.

I want to share with you one of the most amazing and beneficial tools I've learned for not only reducing depression but as a very real way of preventing it. It has to do with our minds. (Surprise!)

What I've learned is not some mysterious secret. It is simply this: how we think has immense power over our mental health and overall well-being.

Interested? Read on.

Whether positive or negative, when we tend to repeat the same sort of mental responses to various situations, we develop *patterns* in our thinking. When those patterns are negative, self-devaluing interpretations of situations, they are *distorted* thinking patterns. Psychologists often use the term cognitive distortions. I call it stinkin' thinkin'.

Each distinctive pattern becomes a choice on a smorgasbord of distinctive, distorted thinking flavors. Each of those choices has the very real potential of being a depression-producing or depression-deepening way of viewing ourselves, our relationships, and the world we live in.

For those of us who love to have lists and categories, there are fifteen different types of stinkin' thinkin':

- filtering,
- black and white thinking,
- overgeneralization,
- mind reading,
- catastrophizing,
- personalization,
- control fallacies,
- fallacy of fairness,
- blaming,
- shoulds,
- emotional reasoning,
- fallacy of change,
- global labeling,
- always being right, and
- heaven's reward fallacy.

I've included brief descriptions of each in the "Additional Helps" section at the end of the book. I think you'll find them quite helpful.

Please don't get overwhelmed or intimidated by trying to figure out which category each of your negative thoughts fall into. Most of us tend to have a few favorites, while others tend to use many of them. Rather than trying to catalogue every thought, I've found it helpful to realize which ones I have a tendency to use. By doing that, it has helped me to recognize what I'm doing when I'm engaged in that flavor of stinkin' thinkin'.

Once you begin to see the patterns in your thinking, you can begin to learn how to stop the distorted thought progression and replace it with a more accurate, equally possible, less-depressing way to think.

I'll be honest; it will take some time and effort to learn how to break those distorted thinking patterns. I recently told someone that it often feels uncomfortable, awkward, or even just plain wrong to think in a new, different, and healthier way. However, it is, oh so, worth the effort and temporary discomfort.

Here is a tried and true four-step approach to breaking and eliminating stinkin' thinkin' patterns.

Oh, before I start, I should mention that it's very helpful to actually write down your responses to each step. It helps clarify what's going on and also serves as a reference for similar thought progressions. You may even want to get yourself a notebook for doing this. I used the work sheets provided in *The Depression Workbook* by Mary Ellen Copeland, MS. It's been around since the early 1990s, but you can still find it on amazon.com.

Okay, the four steps are the following:

o   When you realize that you are experiencing a negative emotion (and sometimes the emotions can be just a

95

faint whisper or subtle twinge), identify the emotion. Am I feeling angry? Insecure? Afraid? Suspicious? Frustrated? Hopeless? Whatever it is, give your best effort in identifying it.

o At that point, describe the situation that produced that emotional response. It's a good idea to be as specific as possible. For example, you'd made arrangements to meet a friend at Lincoln Park on Tuesday at 11:00 a.m. You waited till 11:30 a.m., and that friend didn't show up. On top of that, she didn't respond to your text or voice mail.

o Now, write down what thoughts came to your mind in response. This could range from fearing that your friend had been in a terrible accident (*catastrophizing*) to thinking that you are not really that important to your friend because if you were important, he/she wouldn't have forgotten (*mind reading*).

o Next comes the key in breaking a pattern. Refute the distortedness of your thoughts. In other words, think of other potential reasons that do not reflect negatively on either your friend or yourself. For example, your friend may have gotten stuck in road construction traffic and a meeting that was supposed to have ended by 10:30 p.m. didn't end till 11:30 p.m. You're not making excuses for that friend; you're choosing to give your friend the benefit of the doubt and acknowledging the possibility that there could be a reason other than your initial interpretation(s). Along with recognizing that there could be other reasons comes the opportunity to give yourself suggestions on how to better respond. In this case, that might mean waiting a few more minutes if you have the time. Another option could be sending a follow-up call or text letting your friend know you had to leave but asking to please give you a call so you can reschedule.

Although changing stinkin' thinkin' patterns doesn't happen overnight and you might have to retrain your thought process more than once for the same situation, it can (and will, with practice) become more and more automatic.

Even when depressed, I've discovered that I can change my thoughts to something less...well, depressing.

And that ain't no stinkin' thinkin', my friend.

UNCHAIN MY HEART

Breaking the Addiction
to Emotional Pain

Ever notice how weird it is which things stay strong in your memory? It can be a smell, a song, an event, a turning point in a relationship, or any other of the thousands of things that happen to us each and every day of our lives. Sometimes, it's even an epiphany while lying in bed. That's what happened to me in the blink of an eye close to twenty years ago.

I remember lying on my back, looking up at the ceiling…alone with my thoughts and hurting heart. I remember realizing in an instant of insight that, at some point, I had developed a belief system of sorts. As I looked at it objectively for the first time that day, I saw how fundamentally flawed it was.

I realized in that moment that I had created a philosophy—a theology of how God works—to help me deal with the ongoing, recurring pattern of emotional pain that flavored my life. I had needed something to help make sense of the waves of emotionally painful situations and relationships that didn't point a finger at me saying, "Look how weak, flawed, and malfunctioning you are."

Without realizing it, I had, at some point in my life, created an inner response to that accusation by explaining to my hurting self that emotional pain was evidence of life and growth in my spiritual and emotional being. "No pain, no gain" as the old saying goes, I concluded.

It was then, as I lay in my bed, that it suddenly occurred to me how ridiculous that was. I began to see that in my desire to experience healing from emotional wounds, I was actually unintentionally encouraging pain as validation of my spiritual journey.

I began to realize that I saw myself as an emotional victim, unable to escape pain, so I compensated by putting some sort of ethereal, eternal value on it; if I didn't have times of emotional pain, then it must mean that I wasn't growing and maturing.

Does that seem as ridiculous to you as it still does to me?

I had become addicted to emotional pain, emotional confusion, and emotional upheaval.

So I began to consider the possibility that I could grow and mature without going through emotional crisis. I could learn how to develop a spiritual life that was alive and growing from nurturing it, not subjecting it to being assaulted with pain.

Before I got out of bed that morning, I decided that, although it hadn't been a conscious choice to develop such a warped perspective on my personal spiritual growth, I could consciously choose to replace it with something less traumatic, less depressing.

There was no magic, no fireworks, no burning bush. What there was felt more like…

freedom…

      release…

            peace…

                and

                    optimism.

So how does my moment of emotional enlightenment have anything to do with helping you understand more about depression and symptom management?

For me, emotional crisis has been a willing partner with depression. Emotional crisis can be a vehicle for all sorts of depressive symptoms. As I looked at difficult situations and relationships, all I could see were my failures. Now that's depressing…and more often than not, it can spiral down from there.

From a diagnostic standpoint, depression is a mood disorder. *Hmm*…mood…emotions…pretty easy to see the connection. In fact, my own definition of mood would be an ongoing emotional response to a specific situation or a perception of life in general. I would also venture to say that a mood *disorder* is an emotional reaction that outlives and/or extends beyond its stimulus and becomes an obstacle to a person's healthy functioning in daily life. I know that I'm being overly simplistic, but hopefully, you can see the potential for connections between emotions and depression.

In my journey, my illogical view of emotional pain as a sign of personal growth became an addiction that (falsely) ensured my personal growth. It also served as a diving board into the deep end of depression—not always but sometimes. And I didn't necessarily get to decide when it did or didn't. One of the mysteries of depression is that what you can emotionally handle on one occasion may plummet you down another time.

Facing my addiction to emotional pain and breaking the hold it had on me have been huge benefits to my overall symptom management efforts.

When we live with a wrong belief system about ourselves, it's almost a guarantee that we will be on the losing end of the equation. It's not too surprising that the impact often becomes a shot in the arm for depression.

So my question to you is, "What are you addicted to that is, in reality, a false belief and reinforces wrong thinking about yourself?" Are you addicted to abusive relationships? To failure? To disappointment? To broken dreams? To physical illness? To something else?

I encourage you to consider the possibilities, and if you happen to find some truth, let it set you free. Let it give you a new way of thinking. Let it allow you to break free and give you permission to feel good about life, about possibilities... about yourself.

Many of these issues are so deep that we may need help in correcting them or even identifying them. Sometimes this means professional counseling, sometimes a friend who can be a trustworthy confidante and a source of honest affirmation. Often it can be through prayer and prayer support. Always, it will be through honesty.

And always it will remain your choice whether or not to walk away from whatever gives you reason to not feel good about life. When you make the choice to break free and walk away, you're not a victim anymore. How's that for an epiphany?

Oh, in case you might be wondering...I've found that personal and spiritual growth can and does indeed happen without pain. Not to say that there won't be s-t-r-e t-c-h-i-n-g, but it's not the overwhelming emotional pain that comes from crisis after crisis after crisis.

Yes, I still have occasions—even seasons—where my heart and soul ache beyond what I would ever consciously choose. In fact, those of us who are susceptible to depression also have the capacity for deep emotions. And yes, I still view those times as opportunities to grow. But that's all they are—opportunities that give me a choice and a chance to move forward.

PLEASE DON'T RUN AWAY

The Impact on Relationships

Since I'm not writing this book in any sort of sequential pattern, I don't have to write the chapters in any particular order. Instead, what I have discovered is that the chapters choose when they are written. What that actually means is that I find life presents me with situations (read: challenges) that give me the opportunity to put to practice one or more of the symptom management strategies I had already planned to write about.

So here I am, fully immersed in a situation where I'm on both the giving and receiving end of difficulties in one of my most important relationships.

I have a relative who is currently plagued with a lot of very valid reasons to be overwhelmed with life. Along with a whole shopping cart of medical challenges, it has caused some major depression. As a result, a significant amount of mistrust and paranoia has been plaguing our relationship. In my attempts to help bring accurate understanding of both my words and my motives, I have been increasingly misunderstood, which, in turn, has created more hurt feelings. Then, to complicate things even more, I've also made some very bad choices in how I've communicated; I've gotten extremely frustrated and angry and ended up yelling out my anger and frustration. Not surprisingly, the result has been that I've added to the hurts and misunderstandings. The snowball effect has meant that I have become symptomatic as well. I've been plagued with both anxiety and panic attacks. I have had to fight off the compulsion to bolt and run away from this relationship. I've had trouble sleeping, and I've had to fight off feelings of hopelessness of ever experiencing a healthy restoration of our relationship. We have emotionally wounded each other with our own wounded-ness and we're not out of the woods yet.

Does any of this sound familiar?

There is no denying and, more than likely, no escaping the fact that dealing with depression not only affects the depressed person but affects all those around.

Hopefully, you have at least one or two people in your life who are willing to stand by you through thick and thin, people who accept you, warts and all, through the good, the bad, and the ugly. And yet, even those relationships can be stressed with knowing how to be with you when you're depressed. It's not uncommon for those who care the most to be the brunt of our symptoms. All the while, we may be quite aware that our behavior is pushing people away but, at the same time, behaving in ways that are meant (subconsciously) to alienate us from those who love us. Even in the midst of this destructive behavior, we are crying out, "Please don't run away."

Great, you might be thinking. *If Shelley still doesn't have this down, what are the chances for me?*

In a word…good.

Over the years, I have had fewer and fewer times of interpersonal struggles and hurt such as what is currently going on in my life. As I have learned more about myself and what depression looks like in me and have become more and more consistent in doing what I know to do to manage my symptoms, there has been less and less negative impact on my relationships.

And remember…all significant relationships experience challenges, hurts, and struggles. (That's good news even if it doesn't sound like it.)

What I'm saying here is meant to give you insight and encouragement for learning more about how depression impacts relationships. I'll leave it to someone else to discuss how finances or child rearing or unemployment or the myriad of other life experiences affect relationships. I'm just asking you to remember that no relationship is perfect all the time, in every way.

The other side of the reality coin is that there are practical, tangible things we can do when it's depression that is causing the strain.

In nonconfrontational settings, help those closest to you—your support system—to understand what depression typically looks like, sounds like, and acts like for you.

Help them understand what kinds of things do and don't help during those times. For example, do you recover your emotional stability better or more quickly when you are given space, or does it help to have someone you know cares about you sit with you, not trying to fix you or even trying to make you feel better but just being with you?

I should pause here and mention that you can only have a healthy support system if you choose and nurture relationships that are healthy in and of themselves. It may be obvious, but you can't find healthy support from toxic and/or destructive relationships.

Okay. That's a couple of the basics for how others can help. Now, for what you can do for yourself.

First off, in times of stress of any kind, including the relationship-kind, remember to breathe. Breathe deep and slowly from your gut, not just once, but repeatedly—deep and slow in, deep and slow out.

Trust the words of people who are trustworthy. Give them your permission to let you know if they see symptoms even when you don't. Trust that they are trying to help you when they bring those to your attention. If they say that things will get better, they're not trying to patronize you; they know things *will* get better. Trust their perspective.

A helpful and comforting mental picture that I have used on many occasions is that when I can't tap into my own faith for a situation, I can ride on the wings of the faith of others until my own can sustain me again.

Use what you have learned about breaking distorted thinking patterns. You'll discover or be reminded of what you already know about the importance of replacing irrational/distorted thoughts (and the words that often result) with ones that don't ignore how you are feeling but that reflect a healthier perspective on the subject. (If you haven't read the chapter on breaking distorted thinking patterns, you may want to take a moment and at least briefly look at that subject.)

Here's another example from my own life: In a time of extreme discouragement and feelings of hopelessness, it helped to remind myself of a time when things were better and when things turned out well. Feeling hopeless about the potential to ever again have a good relationship with the relative I've mentioned, I can choose to recall a time of a previous struggle that had been worked through and became stronger because of it.

Notice how the two thoughts are connected? That's essential. If you're feeling discouraged about getting a job, for example, remind yourself of the times you have been successfully employed. What you are doing by that is speaking realistic hope and encouragement to yourself. Doing this can break the power of that sense of hopelessness.

I remember a particular time when my husband and I were dating. I was going through a period of agitated depression (not a pretty sight). It was putting a significant strain on our relationship. As I was making progress in getting my emotional and mental stability back on solid ground (enough to handle his honest answer), I asked him if it made him want to run away when I was like that. I will always cherish his answer. He said, "Wouldn't I already be gone if I was going to?" Yes, he probably already had reason and opportunity enough to run if he was going to, and yet there he was.

We are *never* completely alone. There will always be someone—a person made of flesh and bones just like us— who has not run away. We may feel alone, we may feel rejected, but there's always someone who's still there. We can focus on those who've left or those who remain. The choice is ours. So let's make a habit of remembering to always, always, always be thankful for the people in our life who have not run away and who continue to extend their hearts to us.

WINTER DOESN'T LAST ALL YEAR

The Cycle of Life's Seasons

So "winter doesn't last all year." Wow…news flash. Can you tell me something I don't already know? And what's that got to do with being depressed anyway?

As it turns out…quite a bit.

It was in kindergarten or even earlier when we each began to learn about spring, summer, winter, and fall (a.k.a. autumn). Even growing up in the great Northwest where the seasons often don't look all that much different from each other, they still exist. There are differences—sometimes only subtle—that even children can notice. For me, it was more rain or less rain or whole months of no school or back to school—four distinct seasons.

My first favorite season was summer, mostly because I was tired of being cold. At some point, my favorite switched to autumn. The crunchy colored leaves made me smile, and the crisp air gave me energy. *Aaahh*, fall. As I continued to get older, I eventually started noticing the beauty of spring with all its new life and fresh colors. I wasn't fond of the rain that it took to make it all happen, but I became willing to endure the rain for the purpose it served and the beautiful results. And then there was winter with its months of gray and rain and fog and gray and rain and fog. To add to the unpleasantness for me, the Northwest has that clingy kind of cold that doesn't like to let go of your bones. It took me a very long time to genuinely enjoy winter.

I remember exactly when it happened. My kids were in grade school, and we moved to Colorado Springs, Colorado, where there are four distinct seasons. What I realized was that since winter was going to be substantially different than the other seasons, I needed to own the appropriate clothes. And to think I was an adult with children of my own before I figured this out.

It was from that point (after buying the right clothes) that I gave myself permission to actually like winter. I began to see and enjoy the unique beauty—and value—of each season including winter. I already knew the basics of planting, full bloom, harvest, and dormant preparation, but as I began to appreciate and enjoy the beauty of each, the value and purpose became more and more clear to me as well.

One of our universe's more profound realities is that it's not only the physical world that depends on the existence of all four season, we, as humans, do as well.

You've most likely guessed that my analogy has depression linked to winter, and you're right. But it's more than winter's cold, dreary, seemingly lifelessness that I have in mind.

Winter is a time when life happens under the surface, out of sight. A time of preparation when things must die before new life can begin. We grow in our humanity as we experience and understand the purpose of all the seasons of life.

It's true that depression can seem like a never ending winter of the soul. There are also times when, even without being depressed, life seems flat and dull. Sometimes the biggest challenge is trying to figure out whether or not your particular winter is a strand of the larger web of depression or a winter in one of life's normal cycles of seasons.

In either case, just as it is in nature, the purpose and work of winter is to prepare for greater growth, fruitfulness, productiveness, and beauty in the other seasons of our lives.

Yes, I'm actually saying that there is a purpose and work for depression-related winters. Winter is winter regardless of how or why it comes. I'm a big advocate of using the right tool for the job and the tool or tools you use in any given winter of your soul could potentially vary significantly depending on the underlying cause.

So if your winter stems from an episode of depression, please don't resign yourself to an "Oh well, guess I'll just have to wait for spring and see if I'm still around" attitude.

It's never wrong to do what you can to help alleviate and possibly eliminate the cold, dark cloud that's hovering overhead.

Again, just as in nature, there can be mild winters and harsh ones. Severity and length is not predictable, but we can choose our reactions and actions accordingly.

And take heart...winter doesn't last all year.

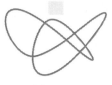

LIGHTING THE FIRE

The Role of Stress

Life is a bonfire.

When I think of bonfires, I think of camping and friends and, of course, s'mores. Bonfires can warm you from an evening chill, cook your breakfast, or burn down an entire forest.

When it comes to depression, a bonfire is less like having a cozy evening with friends and more like an entire forest burning out of control.

So why does depression always sounds so...depressing? Well, probably because it is. Add stress to the mix, and it can feel like your life is going up in flames.

The picture I get of the connection between life and stress is that our everyday life is a process of gathering kindling for that welcoming bonfire. Piece by piece, we lay the kindling down in a pattern that will help the fire to burn just the way we want. It will be big enough to keep us warm but still be able to burn down to a nice bed of coals so that when we're ready for our s'mores, the fire will be ready for the marshmallows.

That would be great if the unexpected addition of stress didn't douse our fire with gasoline and whoosh! It's out of control.

Here's a real-life scenario:

Life is good. You're going about your daily life with all its activities. Your previous depression symptoms are under control, and you're handling the day-to-day responsibilities well. All of life is going smoothly. You can finally have some friends over for dinner. Or perhaps you've been saving your money, and now you can actually take that little mini-vacation you've wanted. Work is going well. You're meeting your deadlines and performing like your old self again. The positive possibilities are endless when you don't have to deal with that old trickster depression and its symptoms.

Suddenly, an unexpected stressor becomes the match that sets all your well-arranged kindling on fire. Before you can blink, your life is on fire, burning out of control.

Your friends are on their way over, the house is clean, and the food prep is on track. Then, in the midst of your visiting, you forget about the cookies in the oven until you catch a whiff of burning chocolate. Taking the cookie sheet out of the oven, you burn your wrist on the edge of the oven rack. It's all downhill from there. Or, perhaps the day before you leave on your mini-vacation, your car breaks down, and it's going to cost you not just your vacation money but eat up your free time as well. The disappointment and frustration drive you over that emotional cliff. Or take the work scenario where the possibilities for unexpected stress are everywhere. Most days you can handle the unexpected—and even handle it well. But on this particular day, the wrench in your plans is overwhelming, and if that wrench was a literal one, you'd throw it across the room before escaping to the nearest closet to finish your tirade in private. Yeah, right…is anything private at your work place?

By the way, have you guessed yet that each of these scenarios has been a real-life situation for me?

Generally, what happens is that I have a meltdown. Get too close to a hot flame, and that's what happens. Another equally accurate picture is me coming out of my firefighting mode looking and feeling like a crispy critter.

After the initial explosion, everything in me shuts down. Old stinkin' thinkin' can reappear, and before I can catch my emotional breath, I'm plummeting downward.

What can make handling stress (I mean handling it *well*) even trickier is that, sometimes, stress produces an invisible flame or even a flame that actually looks manageable, but its slow, steady heat gradually picks up momentum until it becomes a situation where you realize that the fire is spreading faster than you can keep up with it.

Life has a never-ending supply of kindling for our bonfire. So how do we keep life from burning out of control?

Realistically, it's not about eliminating stress. That's mission impossible. The futility of such efforts is just another stressor in disguise. However, there's a lot we can learn to do to *minimize* stress. We can actually develop strategies for managing its negative impact.

At the risk of gagging on metaphors and clichés, with stress management, "an ounce of prevention is worth a pound of cure." And a lot of stress management looks like self-nurturing, so you can read or reread the chapter "Down Time versus Feeling Down" for some preventive medicine for stress hidden in there.

There are also many books, self-tests assessments, and websites that can help us to see where we are at any time on our own personal stress-o-meter. Some things are obvious stressors—death of a friend or close family member, getting married, getting divorced, changing jobs, going on vacation, coming home from vacation, financial difficulties, too much to do, and even not having enough to do.

Those same books and web resources are also rich with stress management strategies. I'm confident that you will find several that you can use and benefit from.

One of my best allies in stress management has been learning to say no. When I feel good, I tend to overcommit. I can't stress enough (no pun intended) the importance of learning, acknowledging, and coming to terms with your limitations. It's okay to not be able to help everyone. It's okay to uncommit if you realize that it's going to be too much.

When it comes to serving others as a way to serve God, I remember when I learned how to be genuinely free from my self-imposed guilt of not doing it all (and by the way, guilt is extremely stressful too).

In a rare back-and-forth prayer conversation, I said to God, "I don't do anything for you."

He replied, "Yes, you do," and then named four or five different roles and activities that I was currently doing that showed my serving heart.

I responded with, "You're right." (I'm sure he was relieved to hear that.) "So why do I feel like I don't do anything?"

His response, "Because you are just now learning what a great debt of love you owe me."

Once again, I replied, "You're right." (Another sigh of heavenly relief was heard, I'm sure). "So how can I ever do enough?"

His answer, "To do what I ask is enough."

I can do that…and you can too.

As we continue to learn what things are ours to do and what are someone else's, we can take a huge weight of stress off our shoulders, stress we were never meant to bear in the first place.

COLORING OUTSIDE THE LINES

Creativity and Depression

Did you know that there's growing evidence that those who are most susceptible to major bouts of depression (bipolar and otherwise) are also some of the most creatively gifted.

Go ahead, get on the internet, and Google "famous people with bipolar disorder" or "famous people with major depressive disorder," and you'll likely be amazed at how many there are…and who some of them are.

Any list of those who have been significantly affected by bipolar disorder or other forms of clinical depression always includes actors, writers, artists, and musicians. Those names would include Ludwig van Beethoven, Patty Duke, Mark Twain, Jimi Hendrix, Vincent Van Gogh, and Edgar Allen Poe. The most sobering example of a life affected by bipolar disorder is Adolph Hitler.

Among others who have had their lives affected by significant periods of clinical depression are Mozart, Michelangelo, Brooke Shields, Martin Luther, Jim Carey, Rodney Dangerfield, Agatha Christie, Winston Churchill, Florence Nightingale, Ted Turner, Ken Griffey, Jr., Abbie Hoffman, and Mike Wallace. Then there's also Marilyn Monroe, Ozzy Osbourne, and Mel Gibson. It can be a very long list.

As you can tell, the link between creativity and depression extends into many more areas than just musicians, painters, and actors. There are sports figures, politicians, astronauts, theologians, mathematicians, and journalists to name some of the others.

It's also pretty obvious that depression doesn't have to prevent success. However, it's a double-edged sword when we also acknowledge that depression can lead to a life cut short or a life riddled with public and private challenges and humiliations.

You might be saying, "So what? I'm not even in the same league as any of the people mentioned." Or maybe you are, and yet there's still the "So what?" bouncing around in your head.

The point here is that if you tend to have bouts of major depression, there's a very good chance that you are also creative. Even if our personal creative potential doesn't put us in the ranks of the famous and gifted people I've mentioned, it doesn't mean there's not a link between our own experiences with depression and creativity.

Once again, you might be very much like I was for a major chunk of my life.

I didn't see my own creative abilities because they didn't fall within my ridiculously narrow definitions.

I couldn't draw. My sister could, so she was the artistic one in my mind.

I could carry a tune but was miles away from being a soloist, so that disqualified me from the vocalist category in my mind.

I liked to write in my diary, but my grandmother was a published author, so I wasn't really a writer.

I love to use color in how I dress and how I decorate my home, but since I would never be asked to design a clothing line or to decorate the White House for Christmas, my abilities didn't qualify me as genuinely creative.

All of that is so wrong—a classic example of my own distorted thinking.

The truth is that creativity is not about performance; it's about perspective. It's about seeing the world through your unique giftedness. It's about dreaming and seeing possibilities that others may not.

Does that make your heart suddenly feel lighter? I'll bet for most of you, it does. And the more you personally embrace an expanded definition of your own creativity, the freer your heart will be.

Now what? Escape to the mountains to write and to paint? Probably not. But we can all learn what our own creativity looks like and how it is essential to our mental health.

With any creative endeavor or artistic pursuit, from park league baseball to major network broadcasting, from singing in the church choir to walking on the moon, it's all about learning to color outside the lines.

You see, the lines, represent the limitations placed on us by either ourselves or others. Move beyond any voices that lead you to believe you're not creative, that you're not talented. Set aside the self-criticism that brings discouragement.

Make time for creativity.

Sing in the shower. Dance in the living room. Work on that invention.

Try new things. Take an art class. Buy a coloring book and crayons. Make some jewelry. Plant a garden. Write with a calligraphy pen.

Or even write a book.

The goal in all of this is not to attain recognition and certainly not perfection; the goal is to liberate and nurture your soul.

Discover or rediscover what you love, and pursue it just for the pure pleasure of it.

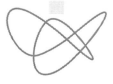

GOOD DAY, SUNSHINE

Getting Outside and Other Helpful Hints

Ever notice how much easier it is to be upbeat when the sun is out?

I grew up in the gray Northwest and remember distinctly how, whenever the sun was out, it felt like I wanted to celebrate. I remember one year in particular when I was walking around the university district on the Fourth of July... in the rain, wondering what in the world I was doing in this dreary place.

I love the Northwest in all its beauty, but from a mental health standpoint, at least for me, I need more sun.

I currently live in rural northern Nevada where it is rare for there to be more than two days in a row where the sun doesn't dominate the sky. It has proven to be good medicine for me...and it's free.

Years ago, I heard that even when the sun is out in all its glory, sitting inside near a window gives you only half the benefits of sunshine compared to actually being outside. Makes sense to me. I don't think Vitamin D penetrates glass, do you?

I've also heard, just recently, that the best benefit from being out in the sun, at least from a vitamin D standpoint, is from about 10:00 a.m. to 3:00 p.m. (or 11:00 a.m. to 4:00 p.m. during daylight savings time). That doesn't mean we go outside and bake for four hours (something I've tried in my youth and now have the wrinkles to prove it). It also doesn't mean that we should avoid other times of the day.

From a depression symptom management perspective, any time of day, any day of the year, sunshine or rain, getting outside is light-years better than staying indoors. (Did you catch my pun, weak as it was? *Light*-years? Sorry.)

Even here in sunny Nevada, I've noticed a distinct change in my frame of mind from just a brief time outside. I can literally feel myself lighten up. (Don't worry; I won't point out the pun again.) A brief time can be even just ten minutes; however, I find that I usually stay out longer once I'm there 'cause it feels so good.

Along with the sunshine, when you're outside, you're very likely moving as well, which enhances the benefit. Walking, gardening, or any movement only adds to the experience. You might even try going to a park and swing on the swings.

Which brings up another helpful hint as my chapter title promised.

Learn to play. Or maybe you already know how to play but have neglected it. Either way, make time for play. Sometimes it's as simple as jumping on the back of your shopping cart while it's rolling toward your car. Drivers beware, adult at play.

Another great "tool" is to have a dog, if possible. If for whatever reason you can't own one, borrow one from a friend or neighbor. Have a doggy sleepover. Dogs are fabulous in their ability to make people feel loved. No allergy excuses either because there are hypoallergenic dogs. We happen to have two: Riley, the Labradoodle who is a thirty-eight-pound mama's boy, and Ralphie, the sixty-five-pound Goldendoodle goofball. I can't begin to tell you how many hours of laughter, comfort, and enjoyment they've given my husband and me.

You don't like dogs? Well, how about a cat? When a cat purrs because you're giving it your attention, you know you are loved. I've even found that a fishbowl or aquarium can be very serene and enjoyable, and dare I say, therapeutic? (One with fish in it works best.)

Let's see, what other hints can I share?

Well, one of my life mottos has become: Take your work seriously, but not yourself. Obviously, this had more application while I was still out in the work world, but it still comes in handy in any situation where a task is becoming more important than my sense of humor.

So there's another hint...nurture your sense of humor. I believe we're all born with a sense of humor. Why else would we have a laugh gene? Want to hear one of my favorite (stupid) jokes? Good. I was hoping you would.

Why is a giraffe's neck so long? Because his head is so far from his body.

Did I at least make you smile? I hope so.

Eat...regularly, as in every three to four hours. Even just a handful of almonds can do the trick. This helps both those of us who don't want to eat and those of us who eat too much. If you have five or six mini-meals, you'll keep your blood sugar much more stable, which not only helps in managing your depression symptoms, but it's also a great way to keep from overeating when you do eat, which in turn helps keep your blood sugar—and your mood—more stable. I call it preventive eating. When you're not depressed, make a list of simple things to have on hand. I already mentioned almonds. There's also string cheese. Yogurt's another good choice, but be sure to check the sugar content when deciding which to buy. My current favorite is Activia's light raspberry. Yum! And if you need some help in remembering to eat, try setting the alarm on your cell phone or, even better, the one on your stove or microwave.

Speaking of alarms...if you're like me, you may have trouble remembering to take your meds. Setting my cell phone alarm to go off twice a day at the meds times has become a great way for me to not forget. It always amazes me that after so many years of taking meds, it's still so easy to forget. If possible, keep your timer near your meds. Once again, if you're like me, you can end up turning off the alarm and not remembering why you had it set to begin with. It's a really good idea to keep at least one backup dose with you as well for those times when you're not at home.

Music is good…really good…for the body, mind, and soul. If you're tense, music can help undo the knots. If you need motivation to clean the house, music can energize. If you're having trouble falling to sleep, soft soothing music or nature sounds can help. If you have disturbing dreams once you are asleep, try listening to recordings of scripture or worship songs as you are drifting off.

If you have other hints that work for you, I'd love to hear about them. After all, we're on this journey together.

BUYING A ONE-WAY TICKET

The Tragedy of Suicide

There's no other way to say it: Depression is a potentially life-threatening condition.

Now where do I go from here? It's an uncomfortable subject, but one that has to be talked about.

When I was in high school, I had no idea that I would ever be diagnosed with clinical depression. And I had never even heard of bipolar disorder or manic depression.

When I was in high school, it was a good twenty years before my "Eight Months on the Sofa."

When I was in high school, I made a promise to God that no matter how I felt, I would never commit suicide. It never occurred to me (well, not until about twenty-five years later) that people who don't struggle with depression don't think of making such promises. Weird, huh?

Well, maybe not weird, maybe more like the grace of God.

There is not a doubt in my mind that it was making that promise that has kept me alive. I've lost track of the numbers of times over the course of my adult life that that promise has kept me from making an attempt to end my life and, quite possibly, succeeding at some point. I wish all my promises to God were so successfully kept. But if there had to be only one promise fully kept, I'm grateful that it was that one.

So suicide has never been an option for me.

Because of that, I also remember many, many times of praying to God (actually, begging God) that he would just take me while I was asleep, that I would go to bed and never wake up...not in this world anyway. However, as I've already talked about in "Winter Doesn't Last All Year," depression passes. And that's a really good reason to be grateful that God doesn't say yes to all our prayers.

If we can each find a way that makes suicide a nonnegotiable, nonoption for us, then it's a nonissue. Right? Well, a nonissue unless someone you love has taken their own life.

Less than two years ago, someone extremely dear to me did take his own life. Along with a large extended family, he left behind a lovely young woman who loved him and a toddler who adored him.

He had addiction issues that had him bound in chains that he had not been able to break free of. Somewhere in the depths of his tormented soul, I believe he came to a point where he fully believed that the only way to keep from hurting the two most important people in his life was to end his life. I can only imagine the pain and agony that he must have felt in the last few moments of his life. My heart breaks for him and for those he left behind.

I firmly believe that taking his life did *not* destine him to hell. He had been introduced to and touched by our Savior, Jesus Christ, and I can envision him in heaven, fully free from the demons that tormented his life here on earth.

Whether you theologically agree with me or not isn't really important. We must each follow our heart's conviction about such things. And if it is the fear of committing the unforgivable sin that keeps you alive, then I approve of your motivation. Not that you need my approval of course but just in case you were curious, I'm just sayin'.

What *is* of the utmost importance is that you discover and use whatever strategies help you choose life no matter how dark and hopeless your life might seem at that point.

So I say it again, please, please find a way to *choose life* no matter what you feel like at any given moment.

If you ever do find yourself at a point where you are considering taking your life, tell someone who cares about you. I don't mean write a note. I mean *tell* someone. Make a promise to that person that you will not attempt to harm yourself without talking to them *first*. You may need to have that person check back with you on a regular basis until you can honestly say the desire to end your life has subsided. If the person who you contacted isn't a mental health professional, you need to make that call as well.

If talking to someone you know is out of the question in your mind, then call a help line. Talk to someone who can't see you and doesn't know you but wants to help you.

Here's a phone number you might want to write down somewhere near your phone or add to your contact list in your cell phone: 1-800-273-TALK (8255). That's the toll free number for the National Suicide Prevention Hotline from their website, wwwsuicidepreventionlifeline.org. You may want to check their website occasionally to make sure that is still their current number. The website also talks about some of the warning signs for suicide. I've included a recap of those warning signs in the "Additional Helps" section. Take the time to become aware of them, and also pass along the info to the people in your personal support system. Do it now so you don't forget, and then live your life as if they'll never need it, okay?

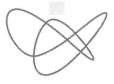

BLUES SKIES ALL AROUND ME

The Reality of Hope

Call it ironic.

    Call it cosmic.

        Call it God.

            Call it a coincidence.

                Call it whatever.

I think I'll call it a chance to practice what I preach.

Four days ago, I had a minor meltdown. Exploded, imploded, I became a picture of the walking wounded. It started out looking like anger (yelling usually does). Over the next hour or so, it settled into what it really was—hurt, extremely painful hurt.

It probably doesn't take much to figure out that it was a relationship crisis with someone I care about very much.

It's been a component of our relationship that, off and on for more years than I should have to admit, I've tried to do what I could to accommodate the other person's physical and/or mental challenges. Whatever the particular consideration, there's been legitimate need and desire to display caring concern and a helping hand. I've failed many times, so it's turned out to be something of a roller coaster ride of its own.

You know the old saying, "The straw that broke the camel's back" or "It was the last straw"? It turns out that the straw doesn't have to be very big; it doesn't have to weigh very much. It can be rather small, almost as light as a feather. But on top of so much other weight, it can have the impact of an anvil.

Somewhere, somehow, with my desire to be everything and anything that would be of help to the other person, I lost sight of my own emotional well-being, and four days ago, it caught up with me. I got a wake-up call regarding boundaries.

So what in the world does this have to do with the reality of hope?

Well, it has become an in-the-moment example that for those of us who are no stranger to depression, even in crisis, there can be hope.

As I have discovered, through these past few days, much to my amazement and gratitude, I'm not depressed!

Hurting? Yes.

Emotionally exhausted? Yes.

Uncertain of what to do next? Yes.

Depressed? No.

How did I figure this out, you ask?

Well, it was more of a revelation rather than a reasoned out conclusion.

Remember, how I mentioned about one of my own early warnings signs being the absence of the song of the day in my head as I wake up in the morning? Yesterday morning, as I awoke to a worship song in my head, I realized that the songs had not stopped in the wake of the relationship crisis. The songs were still there, and maybe not coincidentally, each day's song had been a worship song. Hooray! My heart and spirit were lifted as I've realized this.

The reality is that life isn't perfect...not even close. But the equal reality is that an imperfect life doesn't destine me to slide down into depression's dark pit even during challenging, painful times.

I have been shown a great hope for navigating through life's storms: I can be emotionally and mentally and spiritually well even when I'm hurting. What a gift.

Of course, I should mention that I *did* take steps to take care of myself during these last few days. Later that first day of conflict, I listened to a wise woman suggest that my tears were my heart grieving the realization of what that important relationship has lost over time. So I allowed myself lots of tears. The very next day, I went to church. I was scheduled to be on the worship team, and I chose to go and worship. By doing that, I was able to connect with God in a way that would have been less likely for me than if I had stayed home. The day after that, however, I realized how much my head and entire being were craving quiet. After a short explanation of my need to my husband, I spent the day in the quiet of our bedroom…door closed, TV off. I slept off and on, I read, I prayed, and by the end of the day, I was even playing a little bit of computer solitaire. It was the right thing to do. I wasn't depressed; I was nurturing myself in order to not *get* depressed.

I'm still pondering and praying about how to embrace this relationship in a healthy way so that I don't end up losing it altogether. The overriding word is the need for boundaries… not walls, but boundaries. That's a huge difference. Boundaries establish guidelines for interaction. Walls keep people out. I've resisted contact until my heart is more certain what appropriate, realistic boundaries actually look like in this situation. I'm walking on holy ground so to speak.

And I have hope.

Hope for what?

Hope that I will have God's wisdom and direction and hope that I will not have to walk through depression to get there.

Now, let's change gears and imagine for a moment that either you or I is actually depressed—big time depressed.

Where's the reality of hope then?

It's still there.

If you feel like the sky isn't blue, does that make it any less blue? Of course not. It just makes it harder to see it.

If you live in the Pacific Northwest and you feel like it will never stop raining, does that mean it won't? Of course not.

If you have a cold and you feel like you'll never stop coughing, does that mean you'll spend the rest of your life coughing? Of course not.

If you're depressed and you feel like life will never be worth living, does it mean you'll always be depressed and feel that way? Absolutely not.

The reality is this: depression passes. Sure, it may not pass as quickly as we would like, but it docs, and it will.

That's the reality of hope. Cling to it, count on it, and nurture it.

If you remember anything from this little book, remember—and believe—this:

Hope is not gone.

Hope is not for everyone else except you.

Hope is still there just outside your door.

Go ahead, open the door, and let it in.

ADDITIONAL HELPS

CHAPTERS BY TOPIC

Types of Distorted Thinking

- Filtering/Tunnel Vision: focusing on and magnifying the negative details so that the positives details are filtered out.

- Black and White Thinking: also known as polarized thinking, sees things in an either/or perspective, all or nothing, there is no middle ground (no gray areas).

- Overgeneralization: taking a single unpleasant situation or event as evidence of an absolute, unchanging truth.

- Mind Reading: drawing conclusions about what others are feeling or thinking and why they are acting the way they do, especially when we perceive it to be negatively directed toward ourselves. The most graphic way I've heard this described is "mind rape"— not a pretty analogy, but essentially, we are taking what is private to someone else without their permission or agreement.

- Catastrophizing: imagining the worst case scenario for the outcome in any of life's "what ifs." That's considered maximizing. Minimizing with this type of thinking takes significant events and inappropriately shrinks their significance to tiny-ness, such as with our own desirable traits or accomplishments.

- Personalization: (sometimes called overpersonalization) believing that everything others do or say is meant to—either directly or indirectly—be a negative reaction to you. Unhealthy personalization is also when you compare yourself to others so that you are the lesser. A third type of distorted personalization is *inappropriately* blaming yourself for a negative result and leads to believing that if you would have done something more or something different things would have turned out better.

- Control Fallacies: believing either that you are the victim of circumstances outside of your control or the opposite, that you are responsible for the pain and/or happiness of others; if they're not happy, it must be your fault.

- Fallacy of Fairness: going through life using your own "fairness" measuring ruler against every situation; if the fairness factor doesn't line up according to our standards and expectations, we become negative and resentful.

- Blaming: holding another person responsible for your pain or happiness or blaming yourself for every problem or pain that others experience, which is very similar to one form of personalization.

- The Shoulds: having a list of rules for how both we and others should behave. When we don't live up to our own "shoulds," we feel guilty. When others break our rules, we feel angry, frustrated, and resentful.

- Emotional Reasoning: believing that feelings always reflect the truth. "I feel stupid, unlovable, etc., so it must be true."

- Fallacy of Change: also known as manipulation, expecting that we can convince someone to change in order to suit our needs or desires, believing that our own happiness depends on the other person changing.

- Global Labeling: seeing one or two of our own qualities or errors to extend beyond the context of the specific situation and attaching an unhealthy label on yourself such as "loser." Another form of this type of distortion is "mislabeling" and uses emotionally loaded and negative language to describe the actions of another person. For example, someone is a jerk if that person's behavior rubs you the wrong way.

- Always Being Right: or said differently, always *having to be* right because to be wrong is unthinkable, going to any lengths to convince others that our opinions or actions are correct, which often ends up that our need to be right is more important than the feelings of others.

- Heaven's Reward Fallacy: expecting that any sacrifice or self-denial will be rewarded, and if the reward doesn't come or comes in a different form than expected, then we feel bitter toward others, toward life, and/or toward God.

SUICIDE WARNING SIGNS

The behaviors listed below may mean someone is at risk for suicide. The risk of suicide is even greater if it is a new, untypical behavior or if the behavior has increased. Risk is also greater if the behavior seems to be connected to a loss, significant change, or other painful event.

- Looking for a way to kill oneself, such as searching online or buying a gun
- Talking about feeling hopeless or having no reason to live
- Talking about feeling trapped or in unbearable pain
- Talking about being a burden to others
- Increasing the use of alcohol or drugs
- Acting anxious or agitated; behaving recklessly
- Sleeping too little or too much
- Withdrawing or feeling isolated
- Showing rage or talking about seeking revenge
- Displaying extreme mood swings

SOME OF MY FAVORITE SCRIPTURES

Come to me, all of you who are tired from carrying heavy loads, and I will give you rest. Take my yoke and put it on you, and learn from me, because I am gentle and humble in spirit; and you will find rest. For the yoke I will give you is easy, and the load I will put on you is light. (Matthew 11:28–30, GNT)

Peace I leave with you; My peace I give to you; not as the world gives do I give to you. Do not let your heart be troubled, nor let it be fearful. (John 14:27, NASB)

Not only that, but we rejoice in our sufferings, knowing that suffering produces endurance, and endurance produces character, and character produces hope, and hope does not put us to shame, because God's love has been poured into our hearts through the Holy Spirit who has been given to us. (Romans 5:3–5, ESV)

No, in all these things we are more than conquerors through him who loved us. (Romans 8:37, ESV)

And we know that for those who love God all things work together for good, for those who are called according to his purpose. (Romans 8:28, ESV)

Let your hope keep you joyful, be patient in your troubles, and pray at all times. (Romans 12:12, GNT)

So we fix our eyes not on what is seen, but on what is unseen, since what is seen is temporary, but what is unseen is eternal. (2 Corinthians 4:18, NIV)

Anyone who is joined to Christ is a new being; the old is gone, the new has come. (2 Corinthians 5:17, GNT)

But God's mercy is so abundant, and his love for us is so great, that while we were spiritually dead in our disobedience he brought us to life with Christ. It is by God's grace that you have been saved. (Ephesians 2:4–5, GNT)

And so I am sure that God, who began this good work in you, will carry it on until it is finished on the Day of Christ Jesus. (Philippians 1:6, GNT)

I do not consider that I have made it my own. But one thing I do: forgetting what lies behind and straining forward to what lies ahead. (Philippians 3:13, ESV)

Don't worry about anything, but in all your prayers ask God for what you need, always asking him with a thankful heart. And God's peace, which is far beyond human understanding, will keep your hearts and minds safe in union with Christ Jesus. (Philippians 4:6–7, GNT)

In conclusion, my friends, fill your minds with those things that are good and that deserve praise: things that are true, noble, right, pure, lovely, and honorable. (Philippians 4:8, GNT)

I have the strength to face all conditions by the power that Christ gives me. (Philippians 4:13, GNT)

For God gave us a spirit not of fear but of power and love and self-control. (2 Timothy 1:7, ESV)

Casting all your anxieties on him, because he cares for you. (1 Peter 5:7, ESV)

The Lord is a refuge for the oppressed, a place of safety in times of trouble. Those who know you, Lord, will trust you; you do not abandon anyone who comes to you. (Psalm 9:9–10, GNT)

You, Lord, hear the desire of the afflicted; you encourage them, and you listen to their cry. (Psalm 10:17, NIV)

You make known to me the path of life; in your presence there is fullness of joy; at your right hand are pleasures forevermore. (Psalm 16:11, ESV)

How I love you, Lord! You are my defender. The Lord is my protector; he is my strong fortress. My God is my protection, and with him I am safe. He protects me like a shield; he defends me and keeps me safe. (Psalm 18:1–2, GNT)

The Lord is my shepherd; I have everything I need. He lets me rest in fields of green grass and leads me to quiet pools of fresh water. He gives me new strength. He guides me in the right paths, as he has promised. (Psalm 23:1–3, GNT)

The Lord is my strength and my shield; my heart trusts in him, and he helps me. My heart leaps for joy, and with my song I praise him. (Psalm 28:7, NIV)

I will rejoice and be glad in your steadfast love, because you have seen my affliction; you have known the distress of my soul, and you have not delivered me into the hand of the enemy; you have set my feet in a broad place. (Psalm 31:7–8, ESV)

You are my hiding place; you will protect me from trouble and surround me with songs of deliverance. (Psalm 32:7, NIV)

Cast all your cares on the Lord and he will sustain you; he will never let the righteous be shaken. (Psalm 55:22, NIV)

You, Lord, are forgiving and good, abounding in love to all who call to you. (Psalm 86:5, NIV)

I will say of the Lord, "He is my refuge and my fortress, my God, in whom I trust." (Psalm 91:2, NIV)

He forgives all my sins and heals all my diseases. He keeps me from the grave and blesses me with love and mercy. (Psalm 103:3–4, GNT)

As high as the sky is above the earth, so great is his love for those who honor him. As far as the east is from the west, so far does he remove our sins from us. (Psalm 103:11–12, GNT)

He is near to those who call to him, who call to him with sincerity. He supplies the needs of those who honor him; he hears their cries and saves them. (Psalm 145:18–19, GNT)

Trust in the Lord with all your heart. Never rely on what you think you know. Remember the Lord in everything you do, and he will show you the right way. (Proverbs 3:5–6, GNT)

Have no fear of sudden disaster or of the ruin that overtakes the wicked, for the Lord will be at your side and will keep your foot from being snared. (Proverbs 3:25–26, NIV)

You keep him in perfect peace whose mind is stayed on you, because he trusts in you. (Isaiah 26:3, ESV)

But those who hope in the Lord will renew their strength. They will soar on wings like eagles; they will run and not grow weary, they will walk and not be faint. (Isaiah 40:31, NIV)

Do not fear, for I am with you; Do not anxiously look about you, for I am your God. I will strengthen you, surely I will help you, Surely I will uphold you with My righteous right hand. (Isaiah 41:10, NASB)

Shout for joy, you heavens; rejoice, you earth; burst into song, you mountains! For the Lord comforts his people and will have compassion on his afflicted ones. (Isaiah 49:13, NIV)

For I know the plans I have for you," declares the Lord, "plans to prosper you and not to harm you, plans to give you hope and a future. (Jeremiah 29:11, NIV)

The steadfast love of the Lord never ceases; his mercies never come to an end; they are new every morning; great is your faithfulness. "The Lord is my portion," says my soul, "therefore I will hope in him." (Lamentations 3:22–24, ESV)

The Lord is good, a refuge in times of trouble. He cares for those who trust in him. (Nahum 1:7, NIV)